INTRODUCTION TO

TRIAL ADVOCACY

*How Canadian lawyers prepare for and
conduct civil cases*

JOHN HOLLANDER

A PUBLICATION OF
EST. 2007
ADVOCACY CLUB BOOKS

ISBN 0987707582

ISBN 9780987707581

THE ADVOCACY CLUB BOOKS SERIES

COPYRIGHT NOTICE

TABLE OF CONTENTS

CHAPTER 1: INTRODUCTION TO CIVIL TRIAL ADVOCACY

- *Introduction to trial advocacy*

- *Introduction to the course*

- *The demonstration case*

- *Introduction to the basic techniques*

CIVIL TRIAL ADVOCACY

This chapter introduces the basic concepts of civil trial advocacy and the methodology of this course.

To become proficient advocates, trial lawyers must master two different skills. The first skill required of an advocate is that of case analysis. What is the case about? What does the advocate have to prove? Where can things go wrong? This is a matter of analysis.

The second skill required of an advocate is that of the interview. Direct examinations and cross-examinations are little more than controlled interviews. Of course, the interview is governed by the rules of evidence and the Rules of Civil Procedure, which are taught elsewhere. Nevertheless, it is a steady rhythm of question and answer. The types of question that can be asked may differ as between the different situations of examination. Even so, they are just questions of people and reactions to answers given.

In the adversarial system that makes up the common-law trial procedure, advocates are "officers of the court". This means that they are personally governed by ethical rules that limit the way that they can deal with the witnesses, with each other, with their clients, and with the courts. In Ontario, these can be found in the Rules of Professional Conduct published by the Law Society of Upper Canada.

With that said, a trial is little more than a stage play in which the trial lawyers are responsible for the script. There are witnesses who make up the players. The judge and, occasionally, a jury, are the audience. Unlike a stage play, the transcript comes after the words are spoken out loud.

Seen in that light, two other skills become important. These are the skills of storytelling and case management. Storytelling is a function of case analysis. Once the advocate knows what it is that must be proved in order for the position to succeed, that advocate has to think creatively to present the story in a convincing fashion.

Case management consists of having the witnesses practice their lines, and sorting out who will testify about what and in what order. The trial lawyer must also consider the play that will be put on by the opposition. All of this is governed by the theme and theory of the case that the trial lawyer has scripted.

THE DEMONSTRATION CASE

To show the techniques described in the following chapters, we will use the demonstration case in the appendix attached at the end.

The demonstration case involves a claim that all law students can understand without legal research. It involves the two parties and two other witnesses. It has a couple of exhibits. As all trial lawyers should prepare for every case, it contains a timeline that presents the important dates neutrally as an aide-memoire.

THE BASIC TECHNIQUES

This handbook is not laid out the way a case proceeds.

- It starts with the basics. How trial lawyers think and plan, and how they speak to witnesses.

- Then it proceeds to the examinations, both direct and cross.

- It adds the wrinkles of specific situations, formulaic methods to introduce exhibits, make objections and impeach witnesses during cross-examination.

- It presents opening addresses as an exercise in the balance between storytelling and legal argument.

- It then considers three distinct processes in civil procedure that are not part of civil trials: motions, examinations for discovery and mediation (itself, a course offered in Law School).

- When students prepare to conduct longer examinations, the handbook has chapters on advanced direct and cross-examination techniques and how to deal with experts.

- Then it concludes with closing arguments.

The second chapter will deal with case analysis as such. The thrust of the chapter is to encourage students to gather up all of the information that is available, and then to reduce that information into specific points that make up the essence of the case. Everything that the trial lawyer does must advance those essential elements. Everything else is extraneous, a diversion, a distraction. This chapter introduces the first formula, how to conduct case analysis.

The third chapter will deal with the three different types of questions: the open question, the closed question and the leading question. Each type of question finds its way into examinations of all types. The default choice of law students coming into this course is the closed question. It is rarely the most effective way to ask a question. It reflects the way we think. Unfortunately, this is not the best way to conduct interviews or to persuade. This chapter introduces the second formula, the Magic Formula for successful examinations: short questions with simple language.

The fourth chapter will present the "Five-and-out" formula for examinations and addresses. It focuses the student's attention on the basics of presenting information to an audience. The audience may be the court, the witness, or even the opposition. It introduces the concept of the headline and the necessity to make each point count.

FURTHER READING

The Young Advocates Series (YAS), published by Irwin Law, was written for law students and junior litigators. These are a set of six handbooks.

The handbooks contain many discrete chapters, most with examples and exercises relevant to the chapter topic. Students are encouraged to refer to these handbooks for more detailed discussion than can appear in the following chapters. The subjects covered by the YAS are:

- Interview techniques

- Case analysis

- Discovery techniques

- Professionalism in civil trials

- Mediation

- Legal writing

- Examinations in civil trials (publication pending)

Effectively, this handbook is an introduction to the YAS.

ACKNOWLEDGEMENTS

The author is grateful for the assistance of Professor Stephen Blair, whose guidance contributed much to the ideas communicated in this handbook. As well, the editing prowess of Mary Neill over the Christmas holidays allowed the handbook to be distributed on time.

CHAPTER 2: CASE ANALYSIS AND STORYTELLING

- *The formula for case analysis*

- *How to tell a story*

- *What is meant by the "theory of the case"*

- *The importance of theme*

THE FORMULA FOR CASE ANALYSIS

This chapter introduces the meaning and significance of case analysis. It presents a formula for students to analyze their cases, to see them as litigators do.

Any lawsuit involves a dispute where one side says something different than the other side does. The party that presents its case in a more convincing, more persuasive manner, will likely succeed. Here then is the basic formula:

1. Assemble all of the known facts of the case. Stay neutral.

2. Put the known facts in an appropriate sequence. This is usually, but not always, chronological. Avoid words that evoke an emotional response. Avoid adjectives and adverbs. Stick to neutral facts.

3. Eliminate all of those facts that are not essential to establish the case. This requires knowledge of the legal principles involved. This step creates the

theory of the case. Stated otherwise, *the theory is the list of those elements that make the case successful in law.*

4. Consider the case as a whole. What emotional drivers make this case more convincing than the case of the opposition? *The emotional driver becomes the theme of the case*, as opposed to this theory. Themes are emotional, evocative. Theories are cold and factual.

5. Then review each of the factual elements of the case that make up the theory. Restate these using the emotional driver that is the chosen theme. At this point, adjectives are not only acceptable, they are encouraged. Use evocative words, such as 'crash' to replace the neutral words, such as 'incident'.

6. To complete the theme and theory portion, consider the case from the position of the opposition. Ask yourself these questions:

- What is their theme likely to be?

- How will they present the factual elements in a way that differs from your own case?

- Considering their case and your case, which is more likely to succeed?

- How can you tip the balance in favor of your position?

7. Finally, consider the back story, the personal elements that make your client and witnesses and facts preferable to those of the opposition. These

play to innate biases, perhaps, but they add to the persuasive effect of the story.

STORYTELLING

Once you have the theme and theory, you have to create a convincing way to tell the story. In litigation, unlike in novels, this story is told by witnesses.

That, of course, is not entirely accurate. In fact, advocates get to tell their story at least twice during the course of a case. First is when they make their opening address. Second is when they give their closing argument. Often, counsel have many opportunities during the course of the trial to present or at least support the story, such as during motions. However, all of what they say must be based on what the witnesses and exhibits will say or have said already.

Imagination does not get in the way of presenting the case. Quite the contrary. An advocate has to empathize with the audience: the judge or jury. The story must be convincing to the audience, not to the advocate. For some reason of psychology, counsel usually buy into their own story. The question is whether they can sell it to the audience.

Consider these factors for a successful story:

- It must accommodate the known facts.

- It must represent people the way they typically behave.

- It must explain the unpleasant facts, those that do not seem to support the theme and story that you want to advance.

- It should be packaged in a way that accommodates all of the elements of the theory of the case that are required by law for success.

- It must be provable, such that all of the important elements of the story are provable elements that your witnesses and exhibits can deliver.

- Above all, it must be comprehensible.

When a trial lawyer fixes on a storyline, that lawyer must be able to shorten the story into an elevator speech, one that can be told convincingly between the second and third floors.

Imagine a judge meets you in the hallway and asks, "What is your case about?" What would you say? Can you tell the story that quickly? Can you persuade that quickly? If so, you have what it takes to make a good story.

Just think of the best ads you have seen on TV or heard on radio. Consider what facts the advertiser used to try to persuade you of the merits of that service or product. And all that in the space of an ad slot. Alternately, consider ballads in pop, folk or even rap music. The good songwriter can cover a lot of ground in three minutes. And draw an emotional response.

Tip

When thinking of a story-line, or when preparing a motion, an opening or a closing, always consider the strongest points of the opposition. When preparing a witness for direct examination, consider how that witness will be cross-examined. In short, consider the other side!

THE DEMONSTRATION CASE

How would you look at the demonstration case? It is a straightforward claim, with a few facts and a little law. This is how case analysis would work with this case:

Step one. Assemble the known facts. This has been done in the summary.

Step two. Put the facts into an appropriate sequence.

- Homeowner buys a house.

- Homeowner has and repairs a leaky roof.

- Homeowner lists home for sale, declaring that there are no leaky roof problems.

- Purchaser buys the home, the roof is old, near the end of lifespan.

- Purchaser chooses not to have a professional building inspection.

- Purchaser suffers damage from the leaky roof in first winter.

Step three. We have already eliminated the unnecessary facts. Possibly, too many of them.

Step four. Find the emotional driver. On behalf of the purchaser, the emotional driver could be "Cover-up". In essence, the purchaser will say that the homeowner covered up the defect, hiding a problem that was a ticking time bomb. Passed it on to an unsuspecting purchaser.

Step five. Restate the elements with the emotional driver in mind.

- Homeowner buys a house with a defective roof.

- Defect becomes apparent, causing leaks.

- Homeowner repairs leak, with no visible signs remaining.

- Homeowner lists property for sale, keeping defects secret.

- Purchaser buys home relying upon warranty.

- Damage occurs, in breach of warranty.

- Damage originated in the pre-purchase defect.

Step six. The opposition is likely going to argue that this is a case of contributory negligence. The purchaser had the opportunity to inspect the property so as to detect the problem, but chose not to do so. The emotional phrase might be "Too cheap to buy protection". The issue will be whether the purchaser should have relied upon the warranty, because a professional inspection might well have detected the problem. Alternately, another emotional driver might be "no harm, no foul" because the roof had already outlived its useful life. This was reflected in the purchase price. New roof = higher price. It had to be replaced anyway at approximately the same cost.

It may become important that the real estate agent warned the purchaser to get a professional inspection. The purchaser specifically refused this suggestion. Question: should that fact be one of the elements?

CHAPTER 3: INTERVIEW TECHNIQUES: HOW TO ASK A QUESTION

- *There are three types of questions*

- *Each has its place in interviews, direct and cross-examinations*

- *Avoid closed questions as the default*

- *Open questions and follow-ups require practice*

- *The Magic Formula - Short questions - Simple language*

OPEN QUESTIONS

Let's start with the basics. In order to start a conversation, it is best to use open questions. Typically, these are questions that start with any of these six words: who, what, where, when, why and how. These questions do not limit the scope of the answers. They give free reign to the responder.

By asking a series of open questions, the interviewer allows the witness to tell the story. Words are chosen by the witness, client, or interview subject. These words are not suggested by the question.

Like a blank slate, it may be difficult for the witness to identify what the questioner is looking for. This requires some level of direction on the part of the questioner. This brings us to follow-up questions. These are the direction indicators.

FOLLOW-UP QUESTIONS

Once the open question is asked, the response may be long or short. It may have been unresponsive. Follow-up questions may be in order. Open questions can be asked to follow up what was answered in the initial open question/answer sequence. If the answer was a long one, the questioner can ask a series of targeted open questions to follow up. Consider the following sequence:

Question: Why did you go to the grocery store?

Answer: We had run out of the basics, and needed many things. We had just cashed our weekly paycheck and could afford to go.

Question one: What were the basics that you ran out of?

Question two: Who gave you your paycheck?

Question three: How much was it?

Question four: Where did you cash it?

Tip

The use of follow-up questions is an example of the "broad to narrow" technique. The questioner starts with a broad subject, and then narrows down the subject to the points required for the narrative. Remember this technique when doing your first direct examination presentation in class. It is a good habit to learn.

This next technique is especially good where witnesses are long-winded. It is difficult for an audience, be it judge or jury, to follow a long answer. Lawyers should have the witness focus on what is important for the narrative, rather than just throw words out onto a blank page.

Tip

If the witness gives a long answer, follow up with targeted questions that each use one word or phrase from the long answer. Remember this technique when doing your direct examination presentations in class.

CLOSED QUESTIONS AS THE DEFAULT

A closed question is one to which the answer is either yes or no, right or left, up or down, etc. The witness has very little scope within which to provide information. A typical sequence of closed questions is very boring for the audience, as only the questioner speaks in full sentences, with responses by the witness limited to single words, such as yes or no.

Because stories have to live through the witness who provides the information, the sequence of closed questions is ineffective. Occasional closed questions allow the lawyer to focus on a new subject, or to refocus the witness in an ongoing subject. Only with open questions can a lawyer have the story told persuasively.

One technique in which the closed question is perfectly acceptable is to ask a closed question as the first of the sequence. Consider this example:

Question: Did you attend the meeting?

Answer: Yes, I did.

Question: What happened at the meeting?

From here, the witness gives full details. The purpose of the closed question was to direct the witness to a subject where a long answer would be solicited.

LEADING QUESTIONS

Leading questions are a type of closed question in that the answer must be yes or no. In leading questions, however, the answer is suggested by the question. In a closed question, the answer could be yes or no, left or right, etc. but the answer was not directed. Consider these two examples:

Question one: Did you go to the market on Saturday?

Question two: You went to the market on Saturday, didn't you?

For purposes of control, leading questions are best used in cross-examination. Lawyers are generally forbidden to ask leading questions during direct examinations. There is a common exception, which is described below. There are other exceptions discussed in the later chapter on direct examinations.

The technique of leading questions will be discussed at greater length during the chapter on cross-examination. For the present, just consider that leading questions are not an effective tool to get information communicated. A leading question solicits an admission rather than a story. A sequence of leading questions allows the questioner to present the story, rather than the witness. That is why it is a much more effective tool in cross rather than direct examinations.

It is often said that counsel should never use leading questions in a direct examination. This is not quite accurate. Counsel can lead, and in fact are encouraged to lead, where the subject matter is not controversial.

When discussing a witness's biography, for example, it might be best to lead the witness through a CV. It may be preferable from a tactical point of view to ask open questions about the important areas of the CV, but it will not be a matter of controversy when or where the witness was born, and where the witness went to school.

THE MAGIC FORMULA

You have heard of the KISS principle, about keeping things simple. With interviews and examinations, there is a similar principle. Short questions. Simple language. This is necessary for the witness to understand what is asked.

Short questions rarely have commas or conjunctions. Consider this sequence:

Question: When did you go to school and take math?

Answer: I went to school from age 5 to age 17. I only took math in the last 4 years of that.

The question confused school and math. The answers to each were different. Questions should solicit information about a single subject. While it seems to the examiner that school and math are the same, to the witness they were not. There should have been two questions.

The technique of simple questions is difficult to apply in practice. When we think on our feet, we think first of the concept that we want to accomplish. Only after this do we "translate" this into a question. As a result, the question can be long and convoluted. The witness, audience and lawyer are all confused. In class, the student questioner stumbles and loses both confidence and momentum.

Simple language is a similar technique. We think with the experience of our post-graduate degrees. Often, we are influenced by the evidence we have just heard or read. We should simplify this when we ask questions.

Tip

That is why we make an outline of our questions with enough of a prompt to avoid confusion. It should be short, using simple language. Avoid longer words that can be replaced by simpler ones. "Car", not "vehicle". "Many", not "multiple". We are not asking you to revert to grade 8. We are asking you to make things as easy as possible for your witness (who may only have grade 8) and for the audience.

DEMONSTRATION CASE

Let's look at the witness statement of Alex Homeowner.

Consider these open questions:

Question: When did you buy the property at 123 1st Ave.?

(Possible follow-ups: how much did you pay? With whom did you purchase it? How did you pay for it? What was its condition when you bought it? What inspections did do you do at that time? Who did you have assist you with the inspection?)

Question: What changes did you make to the house after you purchased it?

(Possible follow-ups: when did you make those changes? Who made the changes for you? How much did you pay for them? What photographs did you take? What written plans did you make? What approval did you require from the city?)

Consider this sequence for the closed, then open technique:

Question: Did you suffer any leaks or water damage?

Answer: Yes, I did.

Question: Please tell me about them.

——

Question: Did you repair the leak and the damage to the ceiling in the kitchen?

Answer: Yes, I did.

Question: Please tell me about all of the repairs that you did.

For leading questions, consider each of the previous closed questions (answers are all "yes"):

Question: You suffered a leak from your roof, didn't you?

Question: And the leak caused water damage, didn't it?

Question: You repaired the leak, didn't you?

Question: And you repaired the damage to the ceiling in the kitchen, didn't you?

Question: The repairs left no visible signs of damage remaining, is that right?

CHAPTER 4: FIVE-AND-OUTS: THE MAGIC FORMULA

- *The necessity of outlines*

- *Punchline, headline and five questions or sub-points*

- *The conclusion should suggest itself*

- *Five means several, not many and not necessarily five*

- *One size fits all, as a default structure*

THE NEED FOR OUTLINES

Lawyers love to prepare. We tend to be control freaks. We also tend to think in a linear fashion. This promotes the use of outlines, where we write out what we have to say, argue or write in manageable chunks. Each chunk follows a logical sequence from the introduction to the conclusion. That is how lawyers persuade. It may not be the same with artists, novelists and playwrights, but this is a course for law students.

Consider the formula for case analysis. Start with the earliest fact, and conclude with the punchline. That is a form of outline.

A typical examination, a typical paper, or even a typical opening or closing address, will have an introduction, several relevant points, and a conclusion that wraps it up. From beginning to end, it must be crystal clear.

There are other forms of presentation beyond the simple outline. If these work for you, so be it. Be very attentive to the audience, however. If the audience is a judge, or a law professor, that audience has legal training. Most lawyers think linearly. Juries may be more impressed with the story than with the logical sequence of A-Z. Even so, outlines work for everyone.

ANOTHER MAGIC FORMULA

Start with the point you want to make, which we call the punchline.

Here is the formula for virtually all things that lawyers prepare. Start with a series of points that you want to make. These are the punchlines, as if each were a joke. Write them down. The punchlines are the points that you want to get across.

If you go back to the case analysis, each element is a possible punchline. Quite likely, each element will consist of several points, or punchlines. These are the ones that you have to put into the sequence that will get you logically from the first to the last point of the presentation.

If you want to establish that the grass must be green where the garden starts, then consider all of the points that you have to make in order to get there:

- First, there is a garden.

- Second, beside the garden there is grass.

- Third, the grass changes color with the season.

- Fourth, it was summer at the time in question.

- Fifth, grass is green in the summer.

- Punchline, the grass must be green.

There may be other relevant points. For now, consider that the punchline was that the grass is green, and that the five points in sequence established the punchline.

YOU HAVE FIVE POINTS TO MAKE THE PUNCHLINE

Once you have determined what the point is that you want to make, you have five questions or statements to establish that point. Consider the example of the "grass is green" suggested above. There were five points to be made in order to establish that the grass was green at the time. Each of those could be a statement in a paragraph, or a question in a direct or cross-examination.

HOW MANY IS FIVE?

There is no magic in the number five. The point is to make your punchline in a few points or several points, but not many points. The greater the distance between the start and stop, the more likely that the audience will become confused. The more likely that the witness will become confused. Worse, the more likely that the litigator will become confused.

In the case of long sequences in cross-examinations, often junior litigators argue with the witness. The reason for the argument is simply that the lawyer has lost track of what point was being made. There is always a better way to accomplish the point than to argue with the witness.

The number five, again, is not magic. Just make your point and move onto the next one. That is the rule. Five is just a suggestion. It does sound catchy, though, doesn't it?

HOW TO DELIVER THE PUNCHLINE

When writing or presenting, lawyers have the privilege that they can state the obvious. The sequence of points should make the punchline obvious. It is open to the discretion of the lawyer whether to emphasize that point by stating it out loud.

In the case of direct examinations, to be canvassed in a later chapter, it should be the witness who makes the point and expresses the punchline. This can be accomplished by practicing with the witness. It should not be the lawyer who expresses it.

In cross-examination, also to be canvassed in a later chapter, it should be the sequence of admissions to the questions that make the point and not the witness in a conclusion. The answer to the last question in the sequence, "yes", should be an admission of the point being made. Therefore, the lawyer does not express the punchline. Rather, it is implied by the sequence of admissions made by the witness.

HEADLINES

To compare this to a book, consider that it has several chapters. Each chapter may consist of several headings. The points you want to make will be both the chapters and the headings. The headings will establish the chapter and the chapters will establish the overall point of the case.

We can call them chapter headings or headlines, as in a newspaper. The point here is that it is easy to identify where the questions or points are going if there is a signpost.

- It is very helpful to the audience to know where your questions are leading.

- It is helpful to the witness.

- Where there is a transcript in process, it is helpful to the court reporter.

- It is helpful to the witness in cross-examination, which is why lawyers who practice in the criminal courts do not embrace this technique. In civil trials, however, the advantages far outweigh the disadvantages, as will be canvassed in the later chapter on that subject.

ONE SIZE FITS ALL

By this time, you should consider that you have learned how to make an outline for an address, an examination, or a legal brief.

However, it is just a suggestion, not a straightjacket. The purpose of this formula is to suggest a method to get a task accomplished. There are other ways to prepare a series of questions, or to lay out a presentation. This formula is only suggested as a default for those who need the discipline that flows from following the formula.

Tip

In class, watch your classmates who use this formula, and those who do not. Is the method effective for them? Do you think it is effective for you? If not, try something else.

THE DEMONSTRATION CASE

Let's look at the statement of the purchaser. We will use the five-and-out technique to prepare several questions for direct and for cross. First, the direct examination.

The outline of points, based on the witness statement, might include the search for a house and the purchaser's first attendance at this house.

Each one of these would be the subject of a few questions.

Headline: I will now ask you about your house search.

- Where did you look for houses?

- How many houses do you see?

- With whom did you look at houses?

- What was your price range?

- What other characteristics were you looking for in a prospective house?

- [The punchline is nothing more than that the purchaser was looking to buy a house]

Headline: I will now ask you about the house at 123 1st Ave.

- How did you learn that it was available for sale?

- What arrangements did you make to look at the house?

- Who was there when you went there?

- Tell us about what you saw when you first went into the house?

- Who did you speak with?

- What was going to be the next step?

- [The punchline is nothing more than that the purchaser was introduced to this house]

This demonstrates how five-and-out works in direct examinations. Now let's look at how it might work in cross-examination of the same witness. Again, you would prepare an outline of the points that you want to make in cross. Two of these points are clearly going to be that the agent warned the purchaser to get a building inspection from a professional, which warning he ignored. Consider the following sequence:

Headline: I will now ask you about your discussion with the agent.

- The agent talked to you about the house, correct?

- While you were still in the house, correct?

- And you were told that you could get a building inspection, correct?

- It was suggested that you get a building inspection, correct?

- By a professional building inspector, correct?

- [The punchline is that the agent gave the purchaser good, professional advice. Later, the punchline will be that this advice was ignored.]

Headline: now, I'm going to ask you about what you did before closing the transaction.

- You had signed an agreement of purchase and sale, correct?

- This allowed you to inspect the house, correct?

- And allowed you to bring a professional building inspector with you, correct?

- Which the real estate agent recommended, correct?

- You decided to inspect on your own, correct?

- [The question too many is: Against the agent's advice, correct? The punchline has already been made by the sequence of questions. There is no need to ask the one too many.]

CHAPTER 5: DIRECT EXAMINATIONS

- *The witness tells the story. The lawyer acts as a guide*

- *Open questions are the rule*

- *Keep to the case analysis*

- *Preparation technique*

- *Relative credibility*

PROCEDURE AT CIVIL TRIALS

Civil trials typically follow this procedure:

• The plaintiff's lawyer delivers a brief opening address to introduce the court to what the case will be all about, from the perspective of that side.

• The defendant's lawyer follows with an opening address, highlighting the defence "take" on what the case is about.

• Then it is time for witnesses. Each plaintiff witness testifies in direct examination, questioned by plaintiff's counsel. Cross-examination by defence counsel follows.

• This process repeats until all plaintiff witnesses have testified.

• The plaintiff "rests" and it is the turn of the defence.

• After the last defence witness testifies and is crossed, plaintiffs have the right (rarely exercised) to call witnesses in reply.

• Then it is time for closing argument, first by plaintiff and then by defence counsel.

This chapter deals with direct examinations.

STORYTELLING IN DIRECT EXAMINATIONS

When it comes to testimony of witnesses, the lawyer who calls the witness "directs" or guides the witness through the evidence. After the direct testimony of a witness is completed, then opposing counsel gets the chance to cross-examine.

In the opening address, both counsel tell the court what they expect the story to be from their own perspectives. Then it is up to the witnesses to provide the factual basis for those competing stories. Until the evidence is heard, the stories are just make-believe.

After the evidence has been completed, the stories will either be supported by the evidence or not. If lawyers could agree in advance what the evidence would be, there would be very few trials.

The actual story is told by the witnesses, primarily in direct examinations. The lawyer should guide the witness through the story, to the extent that the witness can contribute. This is where case analysis is so important. Not all witnesses can testify about all elements of the case. It is up to the lawyer who calls the witness to determine where and how the witness can contribute.

Answers should be longer than the questions. It is the tradition of the common-law process for witnesses to explain what happened and the significance of the events. While lawyers would love to tell the story, it is considered to be more persuasive for the witnesses to do so. It is the function of the lawyer to draw this story from the witness in a persuasive way. This is not easy. Trial judges often comment about how difficult it is.

DIRECT TECHNIQUE

The standard technique is for the lawyer to prepare an outline of all of the points that the lawyer wants the witness to make. Then the lawyer addresses each of those points in a proper sequence. The witness testifies about each. In this way, the witness can tell the story, the whole story, and nothing but the story that the lawyer wants presented.

The five-and-out technique works well in direct examinations. The lawyer introduces the subject with a headline. "I will now ask you a few questions about X." The lawyer then asks a few questions about that subject. The witness makes the points that feed the storyline, in the order determined by the lawyer.

In direct examinations, the questions should be open. The later chapter on direct examination techniques presents some specific methods.

After the witness has made the point, then the lawyer introduces another subject. The series of subjects should form some logical sequence, as outlined by the lawyer in preparation for the examination.

A word about evocative language. Lawyers should not use evocative adverbs and adjectives until the witness has used the words. If the witness has described the car as traveling "crazily", it becomes fair game for the lawyer to use the word later in the examination, and during closing argument. The word has been changed from being an opinion to a fact. It is a fact that the witness described the event in that fashion

PREPARATION TECHNIQUE

The preparation for a direct examination is a three-stage effort.

• First, the lawyer reads everything available on the subject, which includes exhibits, transcripts, witness statements and the like. This prepares the lawyer to prepare the star of the show, the witness.

• Second, the lawyer prepares the witness to be examined, a combination of training and rehearsal. By practicing with the witness, the lawyer can acclimate the witness to the nature of the questions to be asked.

• Third, the lawyer prepares for the examination itself. By now, the lawyer is armed with both the documentary evidence and what the witness will likely say. The lawyer prepares an outline of the questions to be asked of the witness. The final version of the outline will accommodate all known factors.

The outline of the lawyer's questions should reflect the case analysis. Again this is constrained by the extent to which the witness has knowledge to contribute. The issues about which the witness can testify may determine the sequence of the direct examination.

THE OUTLINE

The sequence of points may not necessarily be chronological. The two most common formats are chronological and issue-based.

For example, in a traffic accident case it is fair to ask the witness about:

- where the witness was before the accident,

- what the witness was then doing,

- what the witness saw in the accident, and

- what the witness saw after the accident.

As can be seen, this sequence is purely chronological.

For another example, the plaintiff in the same car accident case may be the witness. The sequence might be for the lawyer to ask about:

- where the witness was beforehand,

- what the witness was then doing,

- what damages were suffered in the accident and

- what were the witness's pre-existing medical conditions.

Unlike the earlier example, these questions overlap in time. Each is a separate subject, covering different issues.

There is a major difference between practicing and coaching. In practicing, the lawyer shows the witness what the questions will be. In coaching, the lawyer suggests to the witness what the answers should be. It is that simple. Coaching is unethical.

RELATIVE CREDIBILITY

Witnesses can testify as to what they saw, heard, thought, observed. Often, what they have to say will be contested by other witnesses. In this case, it will be the task of the lawyer to determine whether what this witness has to say is preferable to what other witnesses have to say. This is relative credibility.

Consider the possible reasons:

- This witness was closer.

- This witness made notes.

- The other witness is biased.

- This witness has a better recollection of other things.

- The other witness lied about other things.

There can be many reasons why the testimony of one witness should be preferred over that of another. Lawyers should canvas this during the direct examination of their own witnesses.

Tips

- For the first examinations exercises, keep it simple.

- Use case analysis to make an outline of the main points that you want to establish.

- Stick to the witness statement.

- Then make a list of each fact that you should prove.

- Write down open questions, one per specific subject.

- Divide them into small groups of around five per group, each group making one of the main points.

- If you cannot make the point in a few questions, consider whether you are actually making two points. If so, create a second headline.

- If you feel confident enough to shorten the questions to bullet points of a few words, do so.

- Try not to read the questions, but use your list as a guide.

- Watch the witness as best you can. Rapport is important.

THE DEMONSTRATION CASE

The outline of a direct examination of Brook Purchaser might look like this.

- Experience with houses

- Looked at houses

- Initial inspection

- Purchase offer - exhibit

- Receipt of warranty - exhibit

- Inspection before closing

- Learned of damage

- Repair of damage - exhibit

Each point would be made with a few questions, each introduced by a headline.

CHAPTER 6: CROSS-EXAMINATION

- *The lawyer tells the story through leading questions*

- *Leading questions are the rule*

- *Constructive vs. destructive cross-examination*

- *Keep to the case analysis*

- *Preparation technique*

STORYTELLING AND CROSS-EXAMINATION

Unlike direct examinations, the cross-examiner does not get a chance to practice with the witness. In fact, the witness is likely to distrust the lawyer. If the lawyer suggests white, the witness will answer black. This chapter discusses how the lawyer should deal with the unfriendly witness without the teamwork that is possible in direct examinations.

In the adversarial system, the purpose of cross-examination is to permit the trial lawyer to test the truth or accuracy of what the witness has said in direct examination. Later in this chapter, we will discuss constructive cross-examination, where the lawyer is not trying to break down what the witness has to say, but rather build it up.

Consider these two ways to ask what amounts to the same question:

Question: How did you get to the party?

Answer: I took a taxi, which cost me $25.

Alternate method:

Question: You went to the party, is that correct?

Answer: Yes.

Question: You took a taxi, correct?

Answer: Yes.

Question: It cost you $25, correct?

Answer: Yes.

In the first method, the lawyer gets the witness to answer as best the witness can. With rehearsal, the witness may know to provide the cost. If not, the lawyer can prompt with the follow-up question, "How much did it cost you?"

In cross-examination, this teamwork rarely exists. If the lawyer wants to know each of these facts, then each fact should represent a separate, leading question. In this way, the witness follows where the lawyer leads. There is little scope for the witness to stray from the assigned path. This is a recipe designed for the control-obsessed cross-examiner.

As a story-telling exercise, the first approach is better. The story comes from the witness. The alternate method also tells a story, but it is the questions that contain the story line. All the witness does is agree with what the lawyer suggests. This is not permitted in direct examination. It is to be encouraged in cross-examination.

LEADING QUESTIONS ARE THE ORDER OF THE DAY

Remember the three ways to ask a question: open, closed and leading. If you ask an open question, the witness can take over the momentum of the examination. The answer comes in any which way the witness chooses. The witness can stay on topic, offer explanations, and reconcile apparent differences. This neutralizes the cross-examiner's main weapon: control.

Now consider a closed question, "Did you go to the party?" The witness can say yes or no. The witness is free to venture off of those two choices, to some extent. "Well, neither. It was like this..." And the witness is free to ramble. It is difficult to maintain momentum with closed questions.

Now consider the leading questions that were in the "alternate method" above. There was really not much for the witness to say other than to answer "yes" to each question. That is the ideal for the cross-examiner.

CONSTRUCTIVE CROSS-EXAMINATION

There are times when the witness has something to say that will help the cross-examiner's case. Possibly, the cross-examiner wants to prove a document or fact that only this witness can establish. Who sent the letter? Was it received? Only this witness might know.

Possibly, this witness can support the "relative credibility" of another one of the witnesses to be called by the cross-examiner. There are lots of reasons why the cross-examiner may want positive evidence from the witness under cross-examination.

In that case, the cross-examiner is free to ask open or closed questions. Any way in which the story can be told persuasively is acceptable.

While not strictly speaking true, it is almost as though the witness was called by the cross-examiner. They are allies, at least for this part of the testimony.

PREPARATION AND CASE ANALYSIS

During preparation for the cross-examination, the lawyer should keep to the case analysis. Unlike the theory of the case, however, there is another consideration. That is the matter of credibility. It is common that the cross-examiner wants to attack the credibility of the witness. The witness who cannot be believed on one subject should not be believed on another subject. At least that is the theory.

You should therefore make a list of all of the points in which you, as the cross-examiner, want to score. These would include the following goals:

Attack the points that are in the theory of the case of the opponent.

Support the points that are in your own theory of the case.

Attack the credibility of the witness and of the opponent's witnesses.

Support the credibility of your own party and witnesses.

In your case analysis, there may be some elements of the opposition's case that you do not want to attack. Or, you might decide this witness does not present the right platform to launch an attack.

PREPARATION TECHNIQUE

From your case analysis, you have made a list of all of the points in your theory. You have added points in your opponent's theory. You have taken all of the points together and put them in a sequence that could represent your cross-examination. Now, you do not have to cross-examine on the whole of the theory. Just attack where you can succeed! That is the secret. It is a very poor cross that goes over the whole of the direct, just reinforcing how true it all is.

Then, within each of the points where you can score, think of it as a punchline. How would you introduce the subject? We are looking for a headline here. An example might be, "Now, I will ask you some questions about the intersection." Or, "This brings us to the intersection." You would then ask a few Short Questions (remember the magic formula) to make your point. The answer to each of these should be "yes".

For each of the points that you need to make, you should have in mind a "punchline". Remember the five-and-out technique. You will likely not state the punchline out loud, but it is great if you have one. That is the point that the trial judge should be writing down in the notes of the case. Even better, it is one of the summary points made in the written decision of the trial judge after the trial is decided in your favor.

A WORD OF WARNING ABOUT GRAMMAR

Different cross-examiners use different techniques to phrase their questions. Do they ask a full, grammatical question? Often, senior cross-examiners only make a point, a simple statement. "You crossed the street." Is that even a question? This is not to be risked by junior litigators. There should be a form of question, even if it is only reduced to the short form of "correct" or "right". So, the point becomes, "You crossed the street, is that correct?" The added benefit is that each answer should be "yes", because your suggestion is correct.

Therefore, consider the sequence in the "alternate method" in the party questions above. You can ask the question in any of these ways:

"You went to the party, right?"

"You went to the party, is that right?"

"I suggest that you went to the party. Is that correct?"

All of these are acceptable. If you adopt the statement method without questions, you may not know whether you stepped out of line until the trial judge dresses you down in open court. That is not the preferred method.

Tip

For your first exercise in cross-examination, keep it simple. Try to make five or six points. For each one, introduce a headline, and then ask four or five leading questions. Then move on to the next. Do not try to state that point out loud, especially in your final question of that sequence. That just invites the witness to explain. That explanation may defeat your point. It is known as the "question too many". You will be amazed how long it takes to prepare for a 5 minute cross. With practice, this gets easier.

DEMONSTRATION CASE

We have already looked at examples of the five-and-out in practice in the earlier chapter of that name. Let's look at what an outline of the cross-examination of Kim Contractor would look like. This witness is a quasi-expert, in that it is likely that the witness knows a lot more about the subject matter than does the lawyer.

If we look at the theory of the case, from Chapter 2, what does this witness contribute to the plaintiff? The witness only contributes as to whether there were visible signs remaining on the kitchen ceiling, what damage occurred and causation. Cross-examination should therefore focus on those three subjects. All of the questions provoke the answer, "yes".

Headline: I am now going to ask you questions about what your customer saw at the time of the purchase. You cannot tell whether the ceiling was perfect or not, correct?

- You cannot tell what a professional building inspector would have detected by looking at the ceiling, correct?

- You cannot tell what the purchaser actually looked at, correct?

- [Punchline: because you weren't there]

Headline: now I'm going to ask you about your inspection of the attic.

- You had access to the attic, is that right?

- And you looked into the attic on your first visit to the house, correct?

- The hole in the roof line was visible when you inspected, correct?

- It was readily visible, wasn't it?

- [Punchline: the purchaser should have noticed]

[Note that the last sequence demonstrates "creeping". First, the cross established that the hole was visible. Then it established the hole was readily visible. This is common where a fact could have degrees, such as: far and very far, high and very high, fast and very fast.]

CHAPTER 7: FORMULAE TECHNIQUES DURING EXAMINATIONS: EXHIBITS AND OBJECTIONS

- *Introducing exhibits*

- *Objections*

INTRODUCTION

So much of what litigators do involves formulae. Lawyers have developed certain techniques too that were introduced (in some cases) centuries ago. If it ain't broke, don't fix it, seems to be the rule.

This chapter is devoted to two such formulae. These are encountered in almost every examination. During this course we will drill each of these formulae at every opportunity.

EXHIBITS

There are two main ways to introduce evidence at trial. The first is through testimony of people (witnesses). The second is with documentary or physical evidence (exhibits).

This section deals with exhibits. An exhibit can be a document or a thing. For instance, the glove used in the O.J. Simpson trial was an exhibit. All exhibits are "tendered" for introduction into evidence through a witness or on consent. The tendering process is a formula.

Consider the following sequence:

Question: I am showing you a map. Do you recognize it?

Answer: Yes, I do. I prepared it.

Question: Why?

Answer: I had to report to my superiors about the lay of the land when I performed the surveillance. This map sets out the specific intersection and the other relevant landmarks.

Question: When did you prepare it?

Answer: Shortly after the surveillance was completed.

Statement by examiner: Your Honour, I tender this map as the next exhibit.

The judge: Let this map be marked as Exhibit 14.

The sequence covers all the basics to introduce an exhibit into evidence. Here is the formula:

First, identify the document or thing. This is for the record. "I am holding what appears to be a letter dated January 15, 2014, addressed to you from the University of Ottawa."

Second, show/hand it to the witness. You could do the second step with the first by replacing the word "holding" with the words "showing you".

Third, have the witness identify it.

Fourth, tender the document or thing to the court to be marked as the next exhibit.

Then, the examining lawyer can use the exhibit in the examination.

It is common courtesy, and practice, to give a copy of the document to the opposition in advance. Sometimes, the judge will ask whether that has taken place. It is also possible for the judge to ask the opposing counsel whether the document or thing is to be entered on consent.

There is another common practice; the joint documents brief. Counsel for the parties often agree in advance that some documents should be tendered without objection. Counsel can agree that these need not be identified to be entered. Alternately, they may stipulate that each document only becomes an exhibit when a witness has identified it. Both practices are common.

When could the opposing counsel disagree with the entering of an exhibit? If the document or thing is inflammatory, or if there is some other problem with it - opposing counsel has the opportunity to argue that it is inadmissible for some reason. This takes the form of a voir dire, i.e. with the jury out of the courtroom in a jury trial. The lawyers ask questions of the witness about the proposed exhibit and the judge rules on its admission.

Tip

In this course, we use case studies. They use exhibits. Be prepared to identify them by reference to their respective pages in the materials. Follow the formula each time. Practice with a colleague until you get it right. Like riding a bike, this is a skill you won't forget.

OBJECTIONS

This is not a course in evidence. However, it is a course on trial advocacy, where evidence is introduced. There will be times when counsel takes the position that either a question or an answer, or something else (such as a proposed exhibit), is objectionable. At that stage, there is a form of ritual dance that takes place.

Consider this sequence:

Question: What did the shop clerk tell you?

By opposing counsel: Your Honour, I object. This question calls for hearsay.

The judge: What do you say about that, examining counsel?

By examining counsel: The shop clerk will be testifying shortly. I intend to ask this witness how she reacted to what she was told by the clerk.

The judge: The objection is overruled. Please proceed.

This objection could very well have been successful. It is not a matter for this course to determine whether objections are validly made or not. It is very much a matter for this course to suggest how objections should be made, if the occasion arises.

Note the sequence, which takes the form of a formula:

First, the objecting lawyer stands and states "I object". Then the lawyer gives a brief summary of what the objection is about, such as, "The question calls for hearsay".

At this point, any of several things can happen.

The judge can immediately allow the objection, and direct the examining counsel to rephrase the question or not ask it altogether.

Or, the judge can ask the objecting lawyer for more details about the objection.

Or, the judge can ask the examining lawyer for submissions about why the question should be allowed, or the objection overruled.

What is important by way of courtesy is that only one lawyer stands at a time. Whenever a lawyer addresses the trial judge, that lawyer stands. So you have a little bit of a dance going on. The objecting lawyer rises to make the objection. The examining lawyer sits when that happens. The trial judge addresses one of the lawyers. At that point, the lawyer being addressed rises and the other one sits.

Whatever happens, the lawyers should take it in stride. "Thank you, Your Honour" is a fair response.

For the purpose of this course, only a few types of objection will be recognized. These are identified and explained at the end of this chapter.

TO OBJECT OR NOT TO OBJECT

Tactical objections are those made to disrupt the momentum of examining counsel. These objections have no merit, or are trivial in nature. They are improper and risk sanction by the trial judge.

Lawyers should consider whether the objection is worth the risk of failure. Like video appeals in football and tennis, counsel only get a few chances to try the patience of the judge. If successful, objections make the examining lawyer look bad. If unsuccessful, they reflect poorly on the objector.

If the question or answer is improper, but favorable to the objecting lawyer, there is no cause for that lawyer to object. It is proper for the examining lawyer to interrupt the witness with a direction not to give the answer if it becomes apparent that the answer is likely to be offside. In that case, the examining lawyer should rephrase the question so as to provoke admissible answers. As an example, consider this sequence:

Question: What did you do next?

Answer: I walked to the store, where the clerk told me...

By examining lawyer: Please stop. You may not tell us what you were told.

Tip

If the possible objection involves an important point and might succeed, counsel should be prepared to rise and object. The judge and instructors will respect well-formed objections even when they fail.

DEMONSTRATION CASE

It is likely that the purchaser will introduce the demand letter and the warranty as exhibits during direct examination. Let's try that now:

Question: I am showing you what appears to be a seller warranty disclosure statement. Do you recognize this?

Answer: yes

Question: What can you tell us about it?

Answer: This was given to me by the real estate agent when I visited the house the first time.

Statement by lawyer: I submit this seller warranty disclosure statement as Exhibit 1 to this action. I am handing a second copy up for the use of the court.

Trial judge: The original is to be marked as Exhibit 1.

[At this point, the lawyer hands the document to the court clerk. The clerk stamps the document with the exhibit stamp and enters the description on a list of exhibits. The clerk then hands the document back to the lawyer for use.]

Question: I am now showing you what appears to be a letter written by Lynn Smith to Alex Homeowner. Do you recognize this?

Answer: This letter was sent by my lawyer to the seller on my instruction. I received a copy of it at about the same time it was sent.

By lawyer: I submit this as Exhibit 2 in this action, the letter from Lynn Smith to Alex Homeowner dated June 14, 2015.

During the course of the direct examination of the plaintiff, the following exchange occurs. This demonstrates two of the common objections.

Question: What did the real estate agent tell you when you first visited 123 First Avenue?

Lawyer for the defence: [Stands. Lawyer for the plaintiff sits.] Objection. This calls for hearsay.

Trial judge: What do you have to say about that, counsel for the plaintiff?

Lawyer for the plaintiff: [Stands. Other lawyer sits.] We submit that anything said by the real estate agent was said on behalf of the defendant and is therefore binding and admissible at this time.

Trial judge: I agree. Objection overruled. Please continue, counsel for the plaintiff.

———

Question: The agent told you all about the roof leak, didn't she?

Lawyer for the defendant: [Stands. Lawyer for the plaintiff sits.] Objection. Counsel is leading the witness.

Trial judge: Counsel for the plaintiff, please rephrase your question. Do not lead on matters in issue.

Lawyer for the plaintiff: Yes, your Honour. What did the agent tell you about the roof?

COMMON OBJECTIONS

"Objection, the question calls for the witness to give an opinion."

Evidence is an opinion if it is outside the ordinary experience of a common person. Ordinary people can give an opinion on matters such as speed, height, color, etc. If a witness is asked for an opinion that is outside the ordinary experience of the common person, that witness must be qualified as an expert. This is discussed in a later chapter on experts.

"Objection. This question calls for hearsay."

Evidence is considered hearsay where the witness recounts what another person said. There are several exceptions to the hearsay rule. A common exception is where the words spoken are significant by themselves, regardless of whether they are true.

"Objection. This question calls for the witness to speculate."

A question calls for speculation if it asks the witness to guess.

"Objection. Counsel is leading the witness in an area of importance."

Lawyers may not lead their own witnesses on matters in issue.

CHAPTER 8: IMPEACHMENT OF WITNESSES DURING CROSS-EXAMINATION

- *What is impeachment?*

- *How does it work (the formula)?*

- *Judgment calls*

WHAT IS IMPEACHMENT?

When a lawyer cross-examines a witness, the lawyer may have access to a transcript, documents, or statements from other witnesses. Any of these may contradict what the witness has said during direct examination. Sometimes, the lawyer has evidence that will contradict what the witness now says.

This sets up the sequence for impeachment. "Impeachment" means that the witness's credibility is under attack. Something said earlier contradicts something said currently. The witness's credibility is being "impeached". It is not what is done with the contradiction, which comes later. It is rather the fact of the contradiction that matters at this point. Again, the current evidence must differ from the other evidence. The witness may be innocently mistaken, but need not be lying. Either way, the truth of the testimony is in question.

Consider this sequence:

Question: What color was the barn door at the Ford Farm?

Answer: It was red.

Question: Are you sure?

Answer: Yes.

Question: Do you recall being examined for discovery on October 13 last year?

Answer: Yes, I do.

Question: Do you remember that you were then under oath?

Answer: I was.

Question: I'm going to read to you question 37 from page 18 of the transcript, together with your answer. "Question 37: what color was the barn door at the Ford Farm? Answer: it was blue." Do you remember being asked that question and giving that answer?

Answer: I do.

At this stage the impeachment has been concluded. What the lawyer will do with the contradiction is a matter of a judgment call.

Perhaps the lawyer likes the earlier evidence. The next question should go there. "Would you agree that your earlier answer was accurate?" If the witness disagrees, the lawyer can continue to cross-examine to show why the earlier answer is preferable.

Perhaps the lawyer likes the present evidence. If so, this begs the question, why impeach at all? Let the answer stand, unattacked.

Perhaps the lawyer wants to leave the contradiction in place without further exploration. The witness has said something contradictory to earlier testimony, for whatever that is worth later.

The impeachment formula is a bit of an art form. Students may not be able to master this technique without practice.

Impeachment follows this formula: commit, confirm, credit, confront.

- First, commit. Have the witness commit to the current testimony. If given in the direct examination, have the witness repeat it in cross by asking the same question, or using the words of the witness in a question. "You said in direct that the barn door on the Ford Farm was red. Do I have that right?"

- Second, confirm. Establish the earlier event or circumstance where the witness discussed the same facts. Have the witness confirm that it occurred. Perhaps the witness wrote a letter, diary note or article. Perhaps the witness spoke to a third person, who in turn recorded the statement in a record. Perhaps the witness was examined, in discovery in this case or in another case. "Do you recall being examined...? (or giving the statement, or writing the letter, etc.)?"

- Third, credit. Establish that the earlier circumstance of making the statement was credible, such as being under oath or it being an honest disclosure to the third person. "You were trying your best to be honest at that time, correct?"

- Fourth, confront. Read the contradiction to the witness. Occasionally for dramatic effect, you might have the witness read the letter or note made by the witness. Usually, counsel reads this to control the impact.

Note that this may require the cross-examiner to introduce the other document as an exhibit, if not already entered. "I am showing you what appears to be the letter you sent to Mr. Ford January 15, 2013. Did you send that? Were you being honest in that letter? Your Honour, I tender the letter as the next exhibit."

Guidelines for impeachment include:

- Impeach only where the contradiction is clear. For example, mauve may not be clearly different than purple.

- Impeach only when you can prove the contradiction.

- Impeach when you dislike the current answer.

- Impeach when you want to attack credibility and don't care which answer is accepted.

Impeachment is a difficult skill to master. It requires practice, preparation and thought. When correctly performed, impeachment can change the entire trial. The witness loses credibility, and the case for that witness crumbles. Lawyers' war stories are replete with successful impeachments.

To set up the impeachment, however, the cross-examining lawyer should be ready with the evidence to contradict what the witness has to say. This is time-consuming, and is often not rewarded with a successful impeachment opportunity. Even so, it is something that lawyers should prepare for. This could be the dramatic high point of the cross. Don't waste it fumbling around, looking for documents.

SITUATIONS THAT CALL FOR IMPEACHMENT

- The witness wrote a letter to say X. In direct examination, the witness says something else.

- The witness told the attending doctor or nurse or EMT something, duly recorded in hospital records. In direct examination, the witness says something else.

- The witness made a journal or diary entry. In direct examination, the witness says something else.

- The witness denies doing something at trial. A photo taken before trial shows the witness doing that.

- The witness denies being present at a function. On Facebook, a video shows the witness posed smiling in the midst of the function.

- The witness submitted a CV to an employer, claiming to have a college degree. In direct examination, the witness denies having such education.

- The witness says something at an earlier transcribed examination under oath. In direct examination, the witness says something else.

As in Michael Connelly's novel, **_The Lincoln Lawyer_**, the witness denies in cross-examination having seen the car of the accused. A few questions later, the witness describes that car.

USE OF A TRANSCRIPT WITHOUT IMPEACHING

A common useful technique is to use the transcript of the examination of the witness made at an earlier examination. With the transcript in front of you, ask the questions that were asked in the earlier examination. If the witness deviates from any of those answers, then you have a golden opportunity to impeach.

This is rarely an exercise of pure cross-examination, unless the earlier transcript was done in cross-examination style. Even so, where you like and will rely on the answers given in the earlier transcript, this might be a good technique to adopt.

This technique also works well with a full formal statement made by the witness about the events in question.

BROWNE V. DUNN:

There is a rule of practice in which witnesses are confronted with what other witnesses are likely to say that is contradictory to what the witness is saying or could say. The theory is that the witness on the stand should be confronted with the substance of the expected testimony. If the witness on the stand has not yet discussed the subject, the cross-examiner must raise the subject. Otherwise the witness would have to be recalled at a later time to explain the difference.

Now consider the sequence, which is known by its case precedent name, as <u>Browne v. Dunn</u>:

Question: What color was the barn door at the Ford Farm?

Answer: It was red.

Question: I will be calling Mr. Green to the stand later in this trial. Mr. Green will testify that the barn door was blue at that time. What do you say about that?

This is not, strictly speaking, impeachment. It sets up the dispute between what two (or more) witnesses say so that court can beside which to accept. If the lawyer refers to what a future witness will say, the lawyer must call that witness unless the current witness admits the point.

Answer: Mr. Green is probably correct, then.

Tip

Practice impeachments whenever you get the chance. Try to set them up when you prepare your cross-examination outlines. Have the contradictory source readily at hand. Be ready to commit, confirm, credit and confront. The instructors will reward successful efforts.

DEMONSTRATION CASE

Impeachment does not occur with every witness. Indeed, the opportunity does not arise in every trial. This will demonstrate two examples, one being the common form and the second being the **Browne v. Dunn** situation.

Assume that Alex Homeowner was examined for discovery on October 15, 2015, and gave the answers that are set out in the witness statement. The following exchange takes place during direct examination at trial:

Question: What did the real estate agent discuss with you after the offer to purchase was received from my client?

Answer: She told me that the purchaser was interested in the condition of the roof. I told her that the roof was in decent shape, but that it was quite old.

In cross-examination, the following exchange takes place:

Question: In your direct examination, you said that your real estate agent discussed with you the condition of the roof. Do you recall that?

Answer: Yes, that's what I said.

Question: Do you recall being examined for discovery October 15, 2015?

Answer: Yes, I do.

Question: You were under oath to tell the truth, correct?

Answer: Yes, I suppose I was.

Question: I'm going to read to you the question and answer on the subject given at the examination. [Lawyer reads the question-and-answer]. Do you recall giving that answer to that question?

Answer: Yes, that's what I said.

[At this point, the impeachment is completed. What the cross-examiner chooses to do with it is a matter of strategy.]

The following exchange takes place during cross-examination:

Question: You say that the roof was in good condition, so far as you knew. Is that correct?

Answer: Yes.

Question: The plumber will testify later in this trial that he told you that the roof was not in good condition. What do you say about that?

[The requirement here is that the cross-examiner has the plumber under subpoena and that this is in fact what the plumber intends to say.]

CHAPTER 9: OPENINGS AND STORYTELLING

- *A derivative of case analysis*

- *Application of theme to theory*

- *Based on principles, but juiced by creativity*

- *Openings are constrained by rules*

WHAT IS A STORY?

This should not be so hard to teach. We all know lots of stories. Fairy tales, novels, movie plots, even TV ad spots. Why is it so difficult for law students to grasp this technique? Law students are taught from Day 1 to summarize the case at hand. They are given the plot by somebody else. They pick the salient features from that plot, like they would use a menu. They reduce. They filter out the colour. The remaining elements lead to a conclusion. This becomes the black letter law that students derive from each case. Effectively, it is the theory of the case according to the deciding judge.

This ignores the tension between the parties that led to the case in the first place. The day before the trial, both sides believed that they had a shot to win. After reading what the judge had to say, it may be beyond anybody's imagination why the loser thought so. But, at least as the trial began, the loser had a story to tell that might succeed.

Consider one of your recently assigned court decisions. Or the next one that you read. Pretend that the loser had won. How would the judge have rewritten the story?

THE ART OF STORYTELLING

We can all tell the difference between a good story and a bad one. A good story is one that persuades us of the merits of the protagonist's point of view. A bad story is typically one that we put away, unfinished.

As trial lawyers, the story that springs from a case that we handle comes from a combination of the neutral facts and the spin that we put on those facts. It is our task as litigators to make the position of our clients compelling, persuasive.

How do we do that? This is the art of storytelling. Stories have to accomplish the following:

- They have to accommodate the known facts.

- They have to accommodate the hard facts, the ones that do not favor your position.

- They have to fit within what people ordinarily do.

- They have to evoke some emotional reaction that is either positive for your case, or negative for that of the opposition.

- They have to fit together. By this is meant that the beginning and the end must be linked by a sequence of sensible points. The story must flow.

WHY BOTHER?

Before a lawyer asks a question of a witness, before a lawyer tenders an exhibit, there must be a purpose. That purpose must fit the storyline that the lawyer intends. That makes the lawyer a bit of a screenwriter, where the witnesses are actors who follow a script to some degree.

The lawyer must know how the script reads as the play is being performed by the witnesses. That way, the lawyer can ask sensible questions to accomplish the known purpose.

- What does the lawyer want to emphasize?

- What does the lawyer want to minimize?

- Where are the strengths and weaknesses?

- How can the lawyer bring out the best?

All of these are things that derive from the underlying story.

ENTER CASE ANALYSIS

By this time, it should be obvious that case analysis plays a critically important part in any trial lawyer's practice. Case analysis involves taking all of the elements of the case, reducing them to their bare bones, and then building them up as points that are developed to accentuate the story. Each witness provides evidence in support of the case analysis, the story. Whether the story is sufficiently supported by that evidence depends upon the success of the examinations. It is the object of the opposition to poke holes in that storyline, for that same reason.

One of the challenges for law students when they prepare the storyline is to think outside of their own skin. See the case from the point of view of the opposition, from that of the client, the judge, or another witness. There may be a compelling storyline, if only you can find it. This is worth the effort, as it will inform you on where the weaknesses and strengths are in your case.

Remember the Goldilocks case. For the little girl, the storyline is about child abuse and excessive force. For the Bears, it is about the sanctity of the home and failure of parental control.

All of the lawyers' questions should be directed to establish their respective storyline.

OPENING ADDRESS

The opening address is called an "address" and not an "argument". This is for the reason that it may not contain any argument. Well, what is an argument? An argument puts two positions against each other, advocating one over the other.

This does not mean that you are constrained from presenting what your side of the story is. It also does not prevent you from explaining what the other side of the story is, if that is of help.

Rhetorical questions are permitted. They can serve in place of argument as in:

Our position X is better than their position Y (not acceptable).

The Court will be asked to determine whether position X is better than position Y (acceptable).

An opening address should take into account what the expected evidence will be, whether it will be led by the side of the addressor, or by the opposition. The typical opening address contains the phrase "The evidence will show" or "we anticipate that XYZ will say this..." The reason for this is that lawyers can anticipate, but they cannot be entirely sure. Lawyers should never promise what they cannot deliver.

A typical opening address presents the issue, what the position of the party is with respect to that issue, and where the evidence will lead. It is designed to familiarize the audience (whether judge alone or with a jury) with respect to the case. It should also introduce the audience to the spin that the party intends to put on the evidence to be heard. What will the Court want to decide? How will it do so?

A common opening technique is the following:

"This is a case about invasion of privacy. To succeed, the plaintiffs must show that the defendants entered the plaintiffs' home without consent. The evidence will show that Goldilocks, a child, escaped the care of her parents. She then entered the forest, found the plaintiffs' house and entered it. There is common ground between the parties that there was no consent for this entry."

If documents are part of a joint document brief, as is increasingly common, there is nothing wrong with identifying the documents as if they were admitted into evidence. There has been agreement that they do so, so this is not contentious.

In the opening address, lawyers should avoid controversy except to identify what will be presented in the form of a question. There is nothing wrong with the lawyer asking a rhetorical question that identifies the issue, but does not promise a result.

Consider this technique:

"Should little children be set free to roam and cause damage wherever they choose? Is it not fair that the residents chase the little home invaders, without injury? These are the questions this Court will have to address."

There is a common view that lawyers should not go "over-the-top" in their opening address. They should not play to the emotions of the audience with extreme evocative language. There is nothing wrong with identifying the positions to be taken, but the heartstrings should generally be pulled in closing argument, rather than in the opening address.

To repeat something said earlier, it is important that lawyers not promise what they cannot deliver. When you hear the opening address of the opposition, make note. If the opponent does not deliver what has been promised, this should be one of the main features of your closing argument.

Tip

In the exercises, be very free with your imagination in the storytelling exercise. There are few rules to constrain you. Entertain. Persuade. In the opening address, be much more constrained. You would be amazed by how much you can accomplish in the form of a story or in the form of an opening, in only a few minutes.

Another tip is to look the instructors in the eye as much as possible. Try hard not to read from your notes. This may require practice. The eye contact will be rewarded with better rapport with your audience. Reading out loud is boring. You are trying to animate, not sedate.

DEMONSTRATION CASE

[The idea for the story came from a student in trial advocacy class, using a different case.]

This is a story about an old house. In fact, it is about me, because I am the old house. I was built a long time ago. I am tired. So tired, in fact, that my head is falling apart. My masters have all neglected me. Alex is a pretty good sort, but has no clue about houses. So much so, that while my head is coming apart, nothing is done to keep me together. I remember that I cried so much one day that my tears flooded the kitchen. All that Alex did was mop them up. Nothing else.

One day, Brook pays me a visit. Brook likes me. Brook buys me. But Brook doesn't know that my head is falling apart. Brook looks around and tries to sort out whether anything is wrong with me. Alex lies! Alex says there is nothing wrong with me. Poor Brook. In fact, I am a deeply troubled house. When my head finally falls apart, I start to cry. My tears flood the kitchen. Again. Now Brook knows that I need help. Brook comes to the rescue and saves me.

Compare that to the opening statement that might be made by counsel for the plaintiff:

This case involves a purchaser who bought a home that was defective. The defects were not disclosed to the purchaser, the plaintiff. The seller specifically warranted that "there has been no infiltration by water into the house from the exterior". This warranty was given to the buyer before closing. The buyer relied upon it. After closing, the buyer discovered that there was a defect in the roof that led to water infiltration. It flooded the kitchen. The buyer has suffered damages as a result.

The only question for the court to determine is whether the seller, the defendant, knew that there had been infiltration by water into the house from the exterior. In other words, was the warranty false?

If so, the defendant is liable to reimburse the plaintiff for the damages suffered.

[This opening ignores the case of the defence. At its peril.]

CHAPTER 10: MOTIONS BEFORE TRIAL

- *Technical requirements of the Rules*

- *Follow the form*

- *Case analysis applied to a specific request*

WHAT IS A MOTION?

This course is about advocacy, not civil procedure. Even so, much of an advocate's practice centers on motions. Motions are requests to the court, either a judge or master, for orders (called "relief") in a case. The most common motions are procedural, such as requests to compel a party to produce more documents, to enforce undertakings, to adjourn trials, etc.

HOW ARE MOTIONS BROUGHT?

One party serves the other(s) with a notice of motion, except for those that are brought without notice (ex parte). The motion contains this information:

• When, where and before whom the motion will be heard.

• What order (relief) is sought.

• The grounds for the motion. These are the facts and the Rule that authorizes the motion.

• What evidence the moving party intends to file as part of the motion record. This usually takes the form of affidavits by witnesses to put the necessary evidence before the court.

• The motion record consists of the notice, the affidavits, the exhibits and the pleadings. The responding parties file their own records, but without the notice.

WHAT IS THE ROLE OF ADVOCACY?

Motions are exercises in case analysis. Start with the relevant Rule. What does the moving party have to show to succeed? List the elements required. Then list the facts you can present to establish those elements. Leave out everything else.

Advocacy plays an important role, both oral and written. In most cases, the Court reads the motion record and knows what the result will be. Therefore, lawyers should be careful to phrase their elements so as to put their positions in the best light. These are the attributes of a successful notice of motion:

- It is short, as concise as possible. Judges and masters have to read several of these.

- It is logical. It starts at the relevant beginning and leads directly to the conclusion, without subtlety or detour.

- It uses language that persuades. This should not be "over the top" with descriptive words.

- In other words, it has a point. It makes the point.

ORAL ADVOCACY IN MOTIONS

There is a formula for motion arguments. Effectively, they
follow the notice of motion.

- Identify the order sought, or resisted.

- Identify the relevant Rule.

- List the elements of the Rule that the party must
  establish to succeed.

- Identify the issue that separates the positions of the
  parties.

- Explain how your motion record establishes or
  disproves the necessary elements.

- Explain why your position is better than that of your
  opponent.

- Ask the court if there are questions,

- It is common practice to ask whether the judge or
  master has read the motion records. If the answer is
  yes, counsel can abbreviate several of the steps.

There is not much else to say. Follow the steps. Be concise.
If the Court asks a question, answer it right away. If it is
foremost in the mind of your audience, it should be
foremost in yours, as well.

Sometimes counsel will elect to cross-examine the
deponents of the affidavits filed by the opposition as part of
their records. These proceed much like examinations for
discovery, but are limited to the matters set out in issue by

the motion itself. Lawyers should not expose themselves to such cross-examinations. By filing their own affidavits, they may put solicitor-client privilege at risk.

DEMONSTRATION CASE

The defendant's lawyer writes to Lynn Smith to request a copy of the home insurance policy, which the Rules of Civil Procedure make producible. After two unsuccessful tries, defence counsel brings this motion:

Take notice that the Defendant will make a motion on Tuesday, October 15, 2015, at 10 o'clock in the forenoon before the Court at 161 Elgin St., Ottawa.

The motion is for the following relief:

1. An order directing the Plaintiff to produce a copy of the homeowner's policy of insurance for 123 1st Ave.

2. Costs of this motion.

The grounds for the motion are as follows:

1. The Defendant sold the said property to the Plaintiff.

2. After the sale was completed, the Plaintiff claims to have suffered water damage by reason of leakage from the roof through the ceiling of the kitchen of the property.

3. The Defendant has requested copies of any applicable homeowner's insurance policy.

4. The Plaintiff has neglected or refused to provide such insurance policy.

5. Production of the policy is required by Rule 31.06(4) and the practice of this Court.

The following evidence will be at used in support of the motion:

6. Statement of Claim and Statement of Defence.

7. Affidavit of Alex Homeowner and the exhibits thereto.

Typically, motions such as this are not actually contested. Service of the motion provokes the desired performance. Sometimes, however, there is a reason why the opposition will oppose the motion.

When there is serious opposition, the oral argument at the motion should focus on the reason for the dispute. Notice how bare-bones the "grounds" in the notice of motion are. The argument at the motion itself would focus on the issue before the court. For example, the plaintiff might contend that the motion is premature in that insurance details can be required in the examination for discovery, but not in advance. If so, the argument for the defendant should start with that very issue.

Motions are exercises in case analysis. Notice that the "grounds" omit many of the facts in the case. Because the evidence is limited to the written material presented in advance, there is little scope for embellishment or rhetorical flourish. Motions tend to be boring affairs.

CHAPTER 11: DISCOVERY TECHNIQUES

- *Pre-trial examination of opposing party*

- *Hybrid of direct and cross-examination*

- *Suspension of the "question too many"*

- *Good transcript is part of the goal*

- *Undertakings and exhibits*

WHAT IS DISCOVERY?

Under the Rules, each party may examine all adverse parties before trial. The examination is limited by time. Questions must relate to issues raised in the pleadings. They can be open, closed or leading. The purposes of the examination are:

- It allows the party to know the case of the opposition.

- It reduces the chance for surprise at trial.

- It allows the parties to assess the strength of the witness produced.

- It encourages settlement by allowing the parties to learn (discover) the other side of the story.

- It allows the examining party to try out the theme and theory as a test run for trial.

DISCOVERY TECHNIQUES

Discovery is an exercise in case analysis. The lawyer who conducts a discovery should create an outline of all the elements of the case. It depends on the situation whether the lawyer asks to learn information or to score points.

The fact is that few cases reach trial. There are several steps in which the parties may deal with settlement: negotiations, mediation and pretrial conferences. At these, the discovery may well prove to be the only hard evidence of what witnesses would say at trial.

This suggests that counsel should be willing and prepared to test the case of the opposition, not just to learn it. Of course, counsel can do both in the same session.

USE OF TRANSCRIPTS

The examination is recorded. Transcripts are not mandatory, however. Should the case get to trial, the recording will likely be transcribed. This makes it very important to form questions and sequences of questions with this in mind. The trial judge will not see the demeanour of the witness in discovery. A nod or head shake. A mumbled response. Pauses. These are usually not recorded. They are not meaningful in the transcript if they are recorded. Ambiguous and compound questions lead to useless answers.

Lawyers should ensure that the question is cogent. They should listen to the answer. If it is not responsive, or if it is not intelligible, the lawyer should follow up to ensure that the answer suffices for the transcript.

UNDERTAKINGS AND EXHIBITS

Often, the witness cannot answer some of the questions. In that case, the witness can "undertake" to search records, ask someone else, or otherwise get the information. The witness would then inform the witness's counsel who would send the information to the lawyer conducting the discovery. The transcript should identify exactly what the undertaking covers. If necessary, counsel should repeat the question, using the word "undertake" so that counsel can search for that word in the transcript.

It is common for the documentary productions of a party to be deficient in some respect. When asking about a subject, counsel should also ask whether there are documents that relate to that subject. Counsel should ask for missing documents during the discovery. Sometimes it is helpful to inspect the original of a document, to compare the pen used or to better read poor copies. The request to produce the original should be made in advance of the examination.

Counsel for the witness should not give the undertaking. It is the witness's obligation. Before the witness volunteers to provide information, the lawyer should make sure that the witness can deliver what is promised. There are sanctions in the Rules for failure to comply with undertakings. There are ethical sanctions where lawyers fail to comply with their own undertakings.

THE DEMONSTRATION CASE

A typical examination for discovery might last several hours. It follows a similar outline to the direct examination; however it adds the freedom to cross-examine on points that warrant this tactic.

Let's start this examination for discovery of the plaintiff at the midway point, after the offer to purchase has been accepted. The examining lawyer is the lawyer for the defendant, the seller. Note the five-and-out pattern used.

Question: I am going to ask you some questions about what happened after the agreement of purchase and sale was concluded. What was your first step after receiving the accepted offer to purchase?

Answer: I gave a copy to my lawyer, Lynn Smith.

Question: What discussion did you have with your lawyer with respect to the warranty?

By plaintiff's lawyer: I direct my client not to answer that question on the ground that it is solicitor-client privilege.

Question: Let me rephrase this. What did you plan to do with respect to that warranty?

Answer: I had no plans at all. I simply relied upon it as being accurate.

Question: Now, let's discuss your inspection of 123 1st Ave. I understand that you inspected the property after the agreement was concluded. Is that right?

Answer: Yes, I did.

Question: How did you make arrangements to go to the property?

Answer: I called the same real estate agent who was present during my initial visit. The number was on the listing sheet.

Question: Do you have that sheet?

By plaintiff's lawyer: It is at tab 4 of the productions brief.

Question: I will continue with your plans for the inspection. At this point, was there any discussion of a professional building inspector participating?

Answer: No, there was not.

Question: Did it occur to you then to hire one?

Answer: No.

Question: During the telephone call, what discussion took place apart from arranging the time of meeting?

Answer: Nothing that I can recall.

Question: Now I will ask you some questions about the inspection itself. Tell me about it.

Answer: I met the agent at the door. I went into the property. I looked around. I checked the appliances. I went up to the second floor. The agent came with me wherever I went. I must've had some questions, but I do not recall.

Question: Did you make notes?

Answer: Yes, I did.

Question: They are not in your productions. Would you undertake to produce them?

By plaintiff's lawyer: Do you still have them?

Answer: I may have. I can look.

By plaintiff's lawyer: My client undertakes to use best efforts to locate them. If found, we will produce them.

Question: I will continue with the inspection. Did you look in the attic?

Answer: I do remember that I saw the entry to the attic. I asked the agent what was up there. The agent had no idea. At this point, the agent suggested that I get a professional building inspector to do an inspection.

Question: What did you answer to that suggestion?

Answer: I said that I would think about it. I asked how much it would cost.

Question: What did the agent tell you?

Answer: As I recall, about $1000.

Question: How did that strike you?

Answer: It seemed like a lot of money. I was on a tight budget.

Question: I'm going to ask you now about what you observed during the inspection. I would suggest that the kitchen seemed to be okay, correct?

Answer: Yes.

Question: And you did not notice any repair marks on the ceiling of the kitchen, is that right?

Answer: I did not.

Question: But those marks could've been there, visible to an expert, correct?

Answer: I cannot answer that. I'm not an expert.

[Observe how the flow of the examination proceeds. It is conversational, almost. Note the undertaking. Also note the objection. There is no judge or master present at the examination, so the lawyer for the witness directs the witness not to answer. Usually, the lawyer expresses the ground for the objection. In some jurisdictions, including Ontario, witnesses can answer under protest. This means that the answer is on the record, but cannot be used unless an order is made with respect to it.

Also observe how the discussion moves from open to closed to leading questions, as the tactical situation warrants. In the demonstration, the examiner headlines each sequence of questions. In the final sequence, the examiner had begun a standard five-and-out cross-examination.]

CHAPTER 12: ADVANCED DIRECT EXAMINATION TECHNIQUES

- *Broad to narrow*

- *Looping*

- *Statement with an open question*

- *Breakdowns*

- *Inoculation*

- *Redirect examination*

This chapter suggests several techniques for direct examinations that students should take into account when guiding their witnesses through a direct examination.

BROAD TO NARROW

This technique has the questioner introduce the subject with a broad, open, question. When the witness responds, the questioner uses targeted follow-up questions. These start with who, what, where, when, why and how, to flesh out what evidence is necessary about that particular subject. Then the questioner moves onto the next point.

Consider this sequence:

Question: What happened at the meeting?

The witness then gives a long answer.

Follow-ups as required could include:

- Why did you attend?

- With whom?

- How long did you stay?

- What records did you keep?

- Who did you report to?

Note that each of these sentences is quite short, yet provokes what could be a long answer.

LOOPING

This technique has the questioner use a word or phrase from a previous answer in the next or later question. This technique should be used rarely, as it can be distracting. However, it can be very effective to highlight something important that the witness has said.

For instance, if it is important that the sun was red as it set, and the witness says this, the next question might ask about the "red sun", such as "How did the red sun impress you?"

STATEMENT WITH OPEN QUESTION

To introduce a subject, it is fair for the lawyer to make a brief statement. A brief statement. A few words, or possibly a full sentence. No longer. This would be followed by an open question. Neutral language, please – no controversy allowed here!

For example, the lawyer wants to direct the witness to the intersection at Fifth and Main. The question might be "I understand that an accident took place at the intersection of Fifth and Main. Would you please tell us what you saw?" It should not be controversial that the witness was present. The alternative is a closed question. "Did you see the accident at...?" It is likely not controversial. Either format is acceptable.

CLOSED QUESTION FOLLOWED BY AN OPEN ONE

While closed questions are discouraged in direct examinations, it is fair to ask a closed question to introduce the subject followed by a broad, open one, about the subject introduced.

Consider this sequence:

Question: Were you at the meeting?

Answer: Yes, I was.

Question: Please tell us what happened.

BREAKING DOWN LONG ANSWERS

A very important technique, especially so for long-winded witnesses, is to listen attentively while the witness gives the long answer. At the conclusion, the lawyer should identify each of the important segments of the answer. The lawyer would then use a word, phrase, or concept that was used by the witness in the long answer in follow-up questions.

Consider this sequence, after the witness explains what happened at the dinner table:

Question: You said that your mother interrupted the discussion. What did she have to say?

Answer: ...

Question: You also said that your brother interfered with your explanation. Please explain what happened.

By referencing each of the important aspects of the long answer, the lawyer can accomplish what the witness failed to do, namely inform the audience. The lawyer can also use the technique as a highlighting mechanism for the significant parts of the testimony.

INOCULATION

Just as there are two sides to many stories, there may be weaknesses to what your witness has to say. You cannot simply wish these weaknesses away. You should prepare the witness to be asked those questions that you expect from the opposition. That is part of preparation.

It is also appropriate for you to raise those subjects during the direct examination. This process is called "inoculation". The theory is that it is better to have the witness give the harmful evidence in the least harmful manner under the gentle guidance of directing counsel. Ideally, this sequence has been rehearsed in advance of the examination. The witness can put the best foot forward. In cross-examination, the audience has already heard the story. This may reduce the impact.

Consider these questions:

Question: My friend may ask you whether the sun was in your eyes as you observed the intersection. What do you have to say to this?

Question: It could be said that you were not paying attention during the meeting as it took all of two hours. What do you have to say about this?

Note that these are examples of the "statement with a question" discussed earlier. The question put to the witness is an open one. The purpose of the statement, which cannot be controversial in itself, is to direct to the witness attention to the subject. The examiner should not spin the question. It should be presented neutrally.

REDIRECT EXAMINATION

Although it is not, strictly speaking, part of the direct examination, there is no other spot for us to discuss what happens in redirect examination.

Following cross-examination, the lawyer who called the witness has an opportunity to raise matters that were discussed in cross-examination. Questions asked in redirect should start with the phrase "you were asked about X during cross-examination. Please explain..."

This technique can be used when the witness is not given a chance to explain something by cross-examining counsel. It can also be used when the witness is interrupted. It can also be used, in a desperation play, to give the witness a chance to explain away something that was accomplished during cross-examination.

Tip

In presentations, there may not be enough time to complete the witness. In trials, examinations can take a whole day or longer. Instead of packing every point into the allotted few minutes, make a few points well. The witness's biography is rarely worth the precious time, unless you are part of a team sharing one witness. It is acceptable to explain that time constraints lead you to start at a place other than who the witness is.

DEMONSTRATION CASE

In this direct examination of the plaintiff, we will try out each of the techniques described in this chapter.

Broad to narrow

Question: I'm going to ask you some questions about how you went about finding a house. Tell us about your finding 123 1st Ave.

Answer: Well, I started with the map of the city. I knew about where I was looking to buy. I wanted to live near the canal. I had always wanted a single-family home, and I thought that this would be a good location. I looked in the newspaper for open houses and I went to visit a few. This took two weeks.

Question: Why did you want to live near the canal?

Answer: I had heard that this was an "in" place to live. It was convenient for work, too.

Question: Where did you hear that it was an "in" place to live?

Answer: From my friends and from reading the newspaper.

Question: Why were you interested in a single-family home?

Answer: I did not want close neighbours such as an apartment. I had had some problems in the past and wanted to live in a detached home.

Breakdown

Question: Now, I would like to discuss your experience with houses before this one. Could you please tell us about it?

Answer: Well, I had grown up in one house for most of my life. I knew there was a lot of work, but that was OK with me. I had moved between apartments after I left my parents' home. This was the first time that I was going to live in my own house.

Question: Let me break that down a bit. What type of house did you grow up in?

Answer: A single-family home, much like the one at 123 1st Ave. That is why I liked it so much.

Question: What role did you play at your parents' home with respect to home maintenance?

Answer: None at all. My parents were both handy, and did a lot of home repairs themselves. I did none of them. I was not interested.

Looping

[Follow on from previous questions and answers]

Question: How handy were you?

Answer: Not at all. I just wasn't interested.

Question: Who among your friends was handy?

Answer: None, or at least none that I know of.

Statement with question

Question: Many people learn by watching their parents. What did you learn about home repair from them?

Answer: Not much. At least, nothing that I can recall.

Inoculation

Question: I expect that my friend will ask you why you chose not to hire a professional building inspector. What do you have to say about that?

Answer: It was very expensive. I was on a tight budget. I knew that I could rely upon the warranty.

Redirect examination

[This follows the successful cross-examination with respect to the plaintiff's decision not to look into the attic]

Question: In cross-examination, you testified that you did not look into the attic. Why not?

Answer: Because it would've been no good to me. I didn't know what I would be looking at. I am not handy and it would've been silly to waste the time. And I was relying on the warranty. The seller was the expert in what happened to the house. Not me.

CHAPTER 13: ADVANCED CROSS-EXAMINATION TECHNIQUES

- *Tips for successful cross-examinations*

- *Practice, practice, practice*

- *Watch others*

CONSTRUCTION: LAWYER AT WORK

In the earlier chapter on cross-examination, we discussed the difference between constructive and destructive cross-examination. In constructive mode, the cross-examining lawyer wants to get the witness to provide positive evidence that will assist the case of the cross-examiner.

Because it is the witness who tells the most effective story, the lawyer should be careful to use questions that bring out the story. These may not be leading questions. Open and closed questions may be preferable.

Let's look at some of the examples where a lawyer might switch to constructive mode:

- The lawyer wants to get the witness to identify a document that the lawyer needs as part of the case.

- The lawyer wants to build up the credibility of another witness.

- The lawyer wants to lay the groundwork for a subsequent cross-examination, or impeachment.

- The lawyer has to cover some ground for reasons unrelated to the cross-examination, and does not want to appear hostile while doing so.

- The witness appears to be vulnerable. The lawyer does not want to bully this witness.

There are two times during the cross-examination when constructive mode is most effective. First, early in the cross-examination, the witness may not be as hostile as may be the case later on, as the lawyer scores points. Second, after the lawyer has scored some points, the witness may appear to be sagging. The witness may grab the lifeline of constructive mode and give admissions to soft, open questions that might not be available while the witness is on guard.

PACE AND PAUSE

Cross-examination is all about the lawyer, who should be in total control. Questions should be short, to avoid confusion. They need not be spoken quickly. Lawyers should speak to be understood; in cross as well as everywhere else. The pace of cross-examination is determined by three things:

- The length of the question;

- The complexity of language;

- The pause between the short answer and the next question.

Lawyers should vary their pace to avoid appearing too much of a bully. Judges tire quickly if they have to keep up with a rapid sequence of question, answer, question, answer. Pauses allow the judge a respite to appreciate the point just made.

At the very least, lawyers who use the five-and-out technique during cross should pause after the final answer in each sequence. The judge will more likely get the punchline implied by the last answer.

CONSIDER THE QUESTION

In preparing the outline, the lawyer should take care to get the question right. Even the best preparation leads to miscommunication. When the answer is unexpected, the lawyer should always consider whether to rephrase the question.

ARGUING WITH WITNESS

Lawyers should never argue with witnesses. Such arguments rarely end well. If the witness dodges the question, then the lawyer should rephrase the question or, if necessary, repeat the exact same question. If this is not successful, the lawyer should keep in mind that it might be the question that is flawed, not the witness's answer. To repeat, the lawyer should always consider rephrasing the question as a legitimate alternative.

IMPEACHMENT AS THE RECOURSE

When preparing the outline for the cross-examination, the lawyer should be prepared for the adverse answer. The lawyer wants the answer "yes", but gets the answer "no". The lawyer must have the information, evidence, transcript or whatever, at hand to impeach the client right then and there. That opportunity does not occur often.

Following the sequence in the discovery transcript or witness statement may promote the use of this technique.

THE QUESTION TOO MANY

Once the lawyer has made the point, the lawyer should be careful not to go too far. If the evidence appears not to be reconcilable with earlier answers or with other evidence, the lawyer should not give the witness the opportunity to reconcile apparent discrepancies. Too often, the witness will do exactly that. The fact that the lawyer does not anticipate a reconciliation does not mean that there is none. Don't give the witness the chance.

THE VICTORY LAP

Once the witness has made the concession, or admission, the lawyer should move onto the next point. The lawyer should not repeat or summarize the point triumphantly. If the lawyer takes that chance, then the witness may come to realize what the admission meant. The witness may then backpedal from the previous answer. This might be successful for the witness. The lawyer should never take the chance. The time for the triumphant conclusion is during closing argument, when the witness is off the stand.

WATCH THE JUDGE

A successful cross-examination involves short questions, simple language and one word answers. This can be very difficult for a judge to follow, like rapid-fire from a machine gun. It may be impossible for the judge to make notes. After each point, the lawyer should glance at the judge to make sure that the judge has caught up. The judge's pen is often a clue. If the judge is writing, the lawyer should not ask the next question.

DEMONSTRATION CASE

Let's look at some of the trouble that cross-examiners can get into. We will work with the cross-examination of Kim Contractor.

Arguing with the witness

Question: I am going to ask you about your inspection of 123 1st Ave. in the winter. You got a call from the purchaser, correct?

Answer: Yes.

Question: And you attended at the house?

Answer: Yes, I did.

Question: You saw water coming down from the ceiling of the kitchen, correct?

Answer: Yes.

Question: You did not have to be an engineer to see water coming down, correct?

Answer: Well, of course not.

Question: And you were an engineer, correct?

Answer: What is that supposed to mean?

Argumentative Question: Well, it's obvious, isn't it? You were way over-qualified to fix a ceiling leak, isn't that right?

Answer: Well, that's your opinion. I was just responding to a client's call.

The question too many

Question: I'm going to ask you about your inspection of the roof. You entered the attic from the ceiling in the second floor, correct?

Answer: Yes.

Question: You climbed a ladder near the entryway, correct?

Answer: Yes.

Question: And you opened the entryway and looked into the attic, correct?

Answer: Yes, I did.

Question: You could see a hole in the roof, correct?

Answer: Yes, I could.

Question: Just by poking your head through the entryway?

Answer: Yes, I could.

Question too many: I would suggest that anybody could have done the same and noticed the hole, correct?

Answer: Only if they were qualified engineers and knew what they were going to look for.

Victory lap

Question: You make your living doing building inspections, correct?

Answer: Yes, I do.

Question: And you work for people who are looking to buy homes, correct?

Answer: That is most of what I do.

The victory lap: So, whenever purchasers decide not to conduct inspections through professionals, this keeps you from a sale.

CHAPTER 14: EXPERT WITNESSES

- The formula to qualify the expert witness to give opinions

- The formula for the direct examination

- The secrets of the cross-examination

WHAT IS AN EXPERT?

In the rules of evidence, witnesses may not express an opinion in court. There are two common exceptions:

- Where the subject is familiar to ordinary people, such as estimates of height, distance, speed, and matters of taste.

- Where the witness is an expert in the subject by training, education or experience.

This chapter discusses experts as witnesses. In courses on civil procedure and evidence, students learn more about expert evidence, such as the certification of independence, the requirements for reports and advance notice, etc.

For the purpose of trial advocacy, however, there are three skills that are necessary:

- First, you have to be able to qualify the expert to give the opinion. Occasionally, witnesses can be qualified as such during cross-examination.

- Second, you have to be able to direct the expert, if this is your witness.

- Finally, you have to be able to cross-examine the expert.

QUALIFICATION - THE VOIR DIRE

This is a formula exercise. The witness is called to the stand. In cross, of course, the witness is already there. After identification, the lawyer who wants to tender the witness as an expert leads the witness through the relevant qualifications of education, training and experience. The qualifications phase is a voir dire, in that the testimony and exhibits are conditional upon subsequent acceptance by the trial judge.

Typically, the witness' qualifications are summarized in a résumé or *curriculum vitae* that has been produced in advance. Once identified (or on consent of counsel) the résumé is produced as an exhibit, identified by the witness early in the examination.

THE TENDER

Then, the lawyer tenders the witness as an expert. The lawyer must define the field of expertise that is relevant to the issues in the case. "I tender this witness as an expert in the field of ..." It is important to connect the identified field to the issues in the case. Qualification of an expert in the "field of medicine" may not be not helpful in a case involving complex pulmonary dysfunction, perhaps.

The tendering lawyer should try to assign the narrowest suitable field to the witness' qualifications. It will be up to the judge to accept or reject, or even to modify, this field of expertise. Then it is open for the opposing counsel to cross-examine on the subject only of qualifications. It is common for opposing counsel to concede that the witness should be qualified where it is obviously appropriate.

DISPUTING QUALIFICATION

If there is a dispute over qualifications, the argument takes place after the qualifications cross-examination is concluded. The judge makes the ruling, including the field of expertise for which the opinion evidence is admissible. This sets the boundaries for where counsel can examine (and cross-examine).

Often, opposing counsel concedes the witness' qualification as expert, but reserves questions about expertise for the main cross-examination. The tactic is aimed at showing that the witness is less qualified than another expert in the relevant field.

Tip

When going through the qualifications of the expert, it could be valuable if the witness has been qualified as an expert in other cases. If the witness has published articles or books about the subject matter, it can be helpful to tie the subject of these articles or books to the issues in the case. Similarly, these can be an excellent source of cross-examination.

FORMULA FOR THE DIRECT EXAMINATION

Where there has been an expert report delivered in advance, the direct examination usually follows the outline of the report. Often, so does the direct examination.

- First, the direct examination identifies the area of expertise of the witness.

- Second, it covers the instructions given by the lawyer who called the witness.

- Third, it identifies the nature of issue or question for which the expert's opinion has been solicited.

- Fourth, the expert should provide the opinion. In doing so, the expert should cover the factual assumptions made, research conducted and documents relied on for the opinion.

It is important that the expert establish some level of authority in the courtroom. It is also helpful if the witness can establish rapport with the judge. This requires open questions. It also requires that the expert use simple language. It is far too common for experts to use jargon that loses the trial judge.

Often, there is a fifth area for the direct examination. The expert can explain where the opinion of the opposing expert witness differs (is wrong, or off topic, or otherwise weak). Typically, experts can defend their opinions, and present the weaknesses of the opposing views. This should be discussed with the expert in preparation. It should certainly form part of the direct examination. It can have the same effect as inoculation, but with a witness who is comfortable with the subject matter. This can be a high point on which to conclude the direct examination.

Tip

If the expert uses jargon, or provides a long-winded answer, it is helpful to ask the witness to explain. The direct examination technique of "breakdown" applies here. Listen to the answer. Use the jargon or specific sub-points in the next question, asking for an explanation. "You used the phrase XYZ. What does that mean? [Follow up with:] How does that apply here?"

CROSS-EXAMINING AN EXPERT

Lawyers should be acutely aware that experts have more knowledge about the subject matter than do the lawyers. Therefore in cross-examination, lawyers should be very careful not to argue with well-prepared, confident, expert witnesses. Instead, lawyers should pick their spots. They should find places where the experts are likely to agree. They should find areas where the lawyers know more about the subject matter than do the experts. A likely area for cross is the specific parts of the assumed facts – the factual evidence which can reverse or cast doubt on the opinion.

Typically, the expert has not sat through the entire trial. If the lawyer challenges the facts which the expert has assumed to be true, then the lawyer can be on safe ground. The lawyer has heard the testimony, whereas the expert has not. The expert relies on the facts presented beforehand. These may not be the facts as found by the court.

One valuable technique in cross-examining an expert is that of creeping. Creeping is a technique whereby the lawyer asks about the subject matter in little chunks. The lawyer asks about this one point, for example the weight gain of the party. If that is accomplished, then the lawyer asks a little more about this. And then a little more. If the witness disagrees or challenges at any point, the lawyer can choose to abandon that sequence of questions, without causing any harm.

Consider the following sequence:

Question: You assumed the plaintiff had gained 75 pounds after the accident. Would you change your opinion if the plaintiff had gained only 50 pounds?

Answer: It might do so.

Question: How about 25 pounds? Would that make a difference to your opinion?

This shows that the cross-examiner can approach the subject gently, without diving right in.

THE DEMONSTRATION CASE

We will look at Leslie Expert for the purpose of this review.

The direct examination would follow this outline:

• First, there would be questions about qualifications. Leslie likely qualifies as an expert by reason of being a professional engineer and having experience as a building inspector in cases such as this. Leslie would be tendered as an expert "in the field of home construction and causation of water infiltration".

- Second, there would be questions about what Leslie was asked to do. This is the mandate.

- Third, there would be questions about what information (assumptions, reports, etc.) was given to Leslie as part of the mandate.

- Fourth, there would be questions about what inspections Leslie performed.

- Fifth, there would be questions about Leslie's conclusions and opinions.

- Last, there might be questions about how Kim Contractor could conclude that this was a cover-up.

The cross-examination would reflect the tactical decisions made by counsel.

- How obvious was the hole in the roof?

- Why would a purchaser look there?

- What would a building inspector have seen?

It may well be that this case turns on the warranty and the cover-up, not on the absence of a building inspection. At least, the plaintiff hopes so.

How could qualification of an expert arise in cross-examination? Let's say that Kim Contractor has testified and you (as defence counsel) begin your cross.

Question: You said that you looked into the attic from the entryway, correct?

Answer: Yes.

Question: And noticed the hole in the roof?

Answer: Yes.

Question: Would you say that the hole caused the kitchen water damage?

By Lynn Smith: Objection. This witness has not been qualified as an expert on this issue.

Question: Let me ask you about your qualifications, then... [and so starts the formula to qualify the witness.]

CHAPTER 15: MEDIATION IN CIVIL CASES

- *Controlled negotiation*

- *Confidentiality*

- *How it works*

- *Consider the BATNA*

- *Different form of advocacy*

- *Ethical issues*

MEDIATION IS A FORM OF NEGOTIATION

Law students learn how to analyze, conclude, and report. In that order. More frequently than ever, they are taught to negotiate. Negotiation still does not represent a large part of the curriculum in modern law schools. Even so, this is one of the most important skills for law students to learn as they become lawyers.

Advocacy during negotiation is an art form all by itself. Either in the presence of a mediator or directly between the parties, negotiation is an application of the art of persuasion. It is possible to browbeat your opponent into accepting your point of view. Assuming a level playing field of skills, however, blunt force is rarely a successful strategy. It is usually not in the best interest of the client.

Persuasion in negotiation usually involves acceptance of the weaker elements, with accent on the stronger ones. "Yes, it is true that you have a point to make on this. However, our point on this counteracts that. And we also have this point..."

Typically, mediation allows for a "win-win" situation. Litigation is a negative sum game, in which the legal costs often dwarf the amount of money in issue between the parties. Any settlement may be preferable to continued litigation. That said, lawyers should look at the case from the point of view of their opponents to establish where it is that the other side wants to go. They should then look to their clients' interests: is this settlement offer better than ongoing litigation?

Advocacy during mediation is not advocacy during litigation. Lawyers should consider the conciliatory approach. They should consider the acknowledgement of weaknesses, even when they don't actually see them. The opposition genuinely means what it has to say, and lawyers should acknowledge this. Settlement may be the principal object of the exercise. Keep that in mind. Not necessarily on any terms, but perhaps on terms less severe than the initial position.

Lawyers are hot wired to believe that any form of conciliation is a show of weakness. That is where advocacy plays an important role. Your position may be that your client will win. You must still find a way to acknowledge the chance that the win is in some doubt, either as to likelihood or amount. A win less ongoing legal fees and stress is worth less than a partial win without them. More than this, it is virtually never a sure thing.

Typical insurance cases are payment situations. One side wants to receive money, and the other wants to avoid or minimize the payment. That said, both parties should realize that their positions are not 100% solid. No position is. By pointing out the weaknesses of the opposition's case, the negotiator hopes to soften the position of the opposition. Similarly, that is the goal of the opposition with respect to your position.

In mediation, it is the goal of the mediator (a stranger to the dispute) to keep the parties talking to one another. Mediators want parties to act responsibly. They want them to face up to the weaknesses of their cases. At the same time, they try to provoke settlement offers that narrow the gap between the parties.

CONFIDENTIALITY

What occurs in mediation is protected by privilege, both in common-law and under the Rules. However, something said cannot be unsaid. The opposition will learn whatever you disclose. If your client is willing to accept 50% of the claim and expresses this willingness, the opposition will not likely offer more than 50% later, unless the case changes somewhat.

It is common to demand a greater settlement in light of increased legal costs. Usually, only where the bargaining position has strengthened, will this demand be effective.

HERE IS THE WAY MEDIATION TYPICALLY WORKS.

Beforehand, the parties (through counsel) exchange briefs to express their position. Written advocacy for these briefs is its own topic.

The mediator convenes what is called a "plenary" session. Both parties and their lawyers sit together in a conference room, with the mediator as the convener. After a brief introduction to set the ground rules, the mediator then moves to the next step.

The parties, or more usually their lawyers, make a brief presentation of their respective positions. It is usually best if this is not a strident, browbeating exercise. This is an opportunity for each lawyer to speak to the opposing party, rather than to the party's lawyer. Usually, the lawyer for the opposition cannot and will not be convinced. The party, however, might be.

After the brief exchange of positions, the mediator usually breaks the session into "caucus" sessions. In a caucus, the sides are separated. The mediator shuttles between the two rooms to discuss positions, solicit offers, and tries to poke holes in the position of the party in that caucus room.

If the mediation succeeds, the parties should record their agreement in a contract, referred to as "minutes of settlement". The parties, or their lawyers, or both, should sign these minutes.

Sometimes, the parties resolve some issues but not all. In that case, the minutes would still be the evidence of that agreement.

Should the mediation fail altogether, the mediator files a report to this effect with the court (if mediation was court-connected) and submits an invoice to the lawyers. Parties then go their separate ways and continue the litigation.

BATNA

This is the "best alternative to a negotiated agreement". What will the parties do if they do not resolve the case? The answer usually is ongoing and costly litigation. That is expensive and risky, even in the best of cases. That is the point that the mediator makes during mediation.

THINKING OUT OF THE BOX

Sometimes, it is not only money at stake. One party may be interested in ongoing business, protection of reputation, sales opportunities, a letter of reference or other terms. If there is little cost to one party, and a big benefit to the other, this disparity can be leveraged into a real inducement to settle.

ETHICS

There are several ethical issues in play in mediation. Most important is that the lawyer must put the interest of the client first. If the client instructs the lawyer to make or accept an offer, the lawyer must ensure that the client understands what is involved. Then the lawyer must obey the direction.

Civility is important, as well. Just because a judge is not present, the lawyer does not have free rein to bully the opposing client.

Tip

Law students should shed their partisan cloaks for the mediation exercise. They should demonstrate how they understand the respective themes and theories. They should apply this to encourage a compromise. They should watch the clock. Mediation is often time-limited. There may not be time for baby steps in progressing offers. Your small move may only provoke your opponent's obstinacy.

DEMONSTRATION CASE

Mediation is convened in the offices of Lynn Smith, lawyer for the plaintiff. In attendance are the mediator, the two lawyers and the two parties.

The mediator starts with this presentation:

- The parties are not fighting over very much money.

- The legal costs of the dispute will likely exceed the amount in dispute.

- The parties will not have a future relationship, so it's all about the money.

- That said, what can we do about it?

Lynn Smith makes a presentation making these points:

- His client had no experience with homes.

- There was total reliance on the warranty.

- The warranty was totally wrong, and possibly fraudulent.

- Despite this, Brook wants to resolve the case to save costs and reduce risk.

At this point, the defence lawyer steps in and makes these points:

- Buyers have the obligation to inspect before closing.

- This duty is to retain an expert building inspector.

- A thorough inspection would have disclosed this problem.

- The roof likely needed replacement anyway.

- Brook's case has no chance of success.

The mediator thanks the lawyers for their brief presentations and then separates the parties into their caucuses. The mediator meets first with the plaintiff and Lynn. The mediator makes these points:

- Who cares about the legal dispute? The amount of money is trivial. The roof needed replacement. Do the math and there's nothing at stake.

- The failure to retain a professional inspector could be huge. It could serve as a successful defence or reduce the award due to contributory negligence.

- These risks suggest a compromise is in order.

After some discussion, the plaintiff side says that they will accept $10,000.

The mediator goes to the other room and speaks to defence and counsel. The mediator makes these points:

- The warranty looks pretty ironclad.

- Nobody likes a liar. Will the court find that Alex lied?

- The defence may look bad by trying to wriggle out of the warranty.

- Having said that, the plaintiff will accept $10,000, which looks like a substantial reduction of the claim.

- $10,000 may be less than the legal costs of trial.

After some discussion, the defence responds by saying that they will only pay $5,000. The mediator goes back-and-forth, tries to split the difference a few times and the parties finally settle at $6,650. The parties draw up the minutes of settlement, which the parties sign. The case is settled.

CHAPTER 16: CLOSING ARGUMENT

- *All the evidence is in*

- *Advocate for your client!*

- *Argue why your facts and inferences prove your case*

- *Show why theirs don't!*

- *Watch the judge, not your notes*

THE CLOSING IS AN ARGUMENT, NOT AN ADDRESS

We dealt with the difference between argument and address when discussing the opening address. At the time of closing, lawyers should put forward their very strongest case. Now is the time to connect all the dots between the evidence and the conclusions.

In the argument portion of the closing, you should express the logic behind why your position is better than theirs. Simply put, each of the evidentiary and legal issues to be resolved must now be confronted. It is the purpose of the closing argument to persuade the trial judge (or jury) that your position should prevail.

WHY SHOULD YOUR POSITION PREVAIL?

There are several elements that go into a successful argument. Let's consider some of these:

- Your witness was more credible than theirs.

- You had more and better witnesses to confirm something than they did.

- Your position makes more common sense.

- You can draw inferences from what was not said, or who did not testify. These inferences are favorable to your position.

- You can tell a better story. A better story is one that fits together with all of the evidence. It accommodates what people ordinarily do.

STORYTELLING

Here is where the storytelling exercise comes into play. You have to present your theory, but in a way that resonates with your audience. That is the stuff of storytelling.

Tip

Do good storytellers read from a page or laptop? Well, you shouldn't either. Address the judge (assuming there is no jury). Watch the judge. Is the judge paying attention to you? Is the judge making notes? Don't speak too quickly for the judge to follow. You will score more points with sincerity and rapport than you will lose in fluency. Your notes can serve as a checklist to ensure you don't miss something. They are not a safety blanket.

THE FORMAT OF THE CLOSING ARGUMENT

Foremost in the mind of the lawyer preparing the closing argument is the theory of the case. Has the lawyer proved each of the elements of that theory? Now is the time to put this into some form of structure.

There are several different ways that you can structure your closing argument.

- You can take the case chronologically, starting at whatever you consider the beginning to be. Then you can proceed through the history of the case, interweaving what the different witnesses and exhibits have to contribute.

- Another format choice is by legal issue. Perhaps liability, contributory negligence, economic damages, and general damages.

- In a case involving evidentiary issues, it may be appropriate to focus on specific evidentiary points. For example, who ran the red light? You may have three different witnesses with something to say about this. Ask the rhetorical question, and then provide the evidence of the three witnesses spun the way your position demands.

- Another way to approach the format is to identify what it is you have to prove, your theory. Then identify where the issues are between your and their positions in respect of each element.

THEME

As you recount the elements of your theory, be mindful of your theme. Each element should be phrased in a way that supports your theme. This is equally true when attacking your opponent's theory.

Your theme should support all your elements. A theme that supports some, but not others, may not succeed.

WEAKNESSES

It is very important that you confront the weaknesses of your position and the strengths of the position of your opponent. If you do not, you leave the judge to sort this out alone. Worse, the judge will be assisted by your opponent only. Deal with these weaknesses. You can interweave them into your structure, or you can have a separate section devoted exclusively to the "hard points".

CHOICE OF LANGUAGE

Descriptive words are best not used during the trial until used by witnesses. During closing argument, however, counsel is free to describe events, facts, witnesses, with any descriptive language that they want. They should not go "over-the-top", but the actual boundary will differ from lawyer to lawyer.

As should have been true throughout the trial, however, lawyers should continue to use the simplest language possible. Judges are familiar with complex language. Even so, simple language is the most persuasive.

BE TRUE TO YOURSELF

Law school is certainly the time to try out new techniques. By this time you will have a good idea about your own character. Are you adventuresome? Are you willing to take risks? Are you flamboyant? Are you at your best when you present with little emotion (a "flat affect", to psychologists)? Consider the difference between the speaking methods of Candidate Barak Obama on the campaign trail and those of President Obama in the White House. Different times call for different tactics.

Some law students are very professorial when they give their closing argument. Some are prone to flights of fancy and rhetoric. Whatever your particular personality, this should be reflected by the closing argument. If you try to be something that you are not, this may well show up in the way you present.

TRY TO FINISH WITH A GOOD LINE

Your last point should connect the relief asked to the theme you have pressed in the trial (and in the closing). Why should your position prevail? It should be more than just the money. It should be about righting some wrong - or avoiding one.

THE DEMONSTRATION CASE

On behalf of the defendant, this might be a closing argument. Note that it combines theme and theory in a storytelling mode.

The plaintiff would have the court accept that this is a case of breach of warranty. Far from it. This is a case about a purchaser who was too cheap to pay for the minimal protection required by law.

It is common ground between the parties what happened. The defendant owned the house, an old house. There was no secret about that. The purchaser came to look at the house. The purchaser bought the old house, paid for an old house and got exactly what was bargained for.

It is common ground that the seller gave a warranty. It is arguable whether the warranty was breached. That actually does not matter. What is common ground is that the purchaser chose not to do a thorough inspection" the purchaser chose not to hire a building inspector.

The real estate agent specifically told the purchaser to get a professional building inspection. The purchaser admits to being inept in these matters. The purchaser did not even bother to look into the attic. The purchaser consulted a lawyer, Lynn Smith, before closing. We do not know what the lawyer told the plaintiff to do, because the plaintiff is hiding behind solicitor-client secrecy. An inference can be drawn that the lawyer suggested that the plaintiff get a building inspection.

The evidence of both the plaintiff's contractor and the defendant's expert suggest that a prudent inspection would have discovered this flaw in the roof. This flaw caused the kitchen problems. It is common ground that the purchaser is bound by whatever a thorough inspection would have uncovered. That should be the end of the case.

In the end, the plaintiff gets a new roof that was going to be necessary soon in any event, as the roof was old. The price was a little more than would have been the case otherwise. No harm, no foul.

As I said earlier, this is not a case of breach of warranty. The only excuse that the plaintiff has for not getting a building inspection performed by a professional is that it cost $1,000. Well, compare that to the price of the home. Compare that to the costs of this litigation. This is a case of a purchaser who was too cheap to cover the essential basics required by law. The defendant submits that this action should be dismissed with cost payable to the defendant.

APPENDIX A: LATENT DEFECT CASE SUMMARY

This is a case about water damage that was caused to the ceiling of the kitchen in an old house. The homeowner has owned the house for 20 years. During the time of ownership, water came through the roof into the attic, and then followed a duct into the ceiling of the kitchen on the ground floor. Water dripped from the ceiling of the kitchen onto the wood floor. The homeowner had to replace the wood floor, and chose to do so with ceramic tile. The ceiling was patched and repainted. There was no evident ("patent") damage.

During the listing of the property for sale, the homeowner signed a disclosure statement that stated there was no water damage suffered by the house during the homeowner's ownership. The purchaser took possession of the property after a cursory inspection. The inspection identified that the roof was 20 years old. The roofing industry has 30 year warranties for the type of roof in question.

Six months after the closing, in a particularly severe winter, there was water found dripping from the ceiling. The purchaser retained a contractor who detected that this was caused by a leak in the roof. A review of the source of the leak showed that this was something that had occurred in the past.

The purchaser sues the homeowner for damages arising from repairs necessary to the roof and to the ceiling.

Legal regime

The law provides that the homeowner has to reveal latent, or hidden, defects of which the owner actually knows. The law requires that purchasers undertake thorough building inspections, failing which they are deemed to have done so. They cannot claim for any defect that a thorough inspection would have disclosed. The law also requires full and frank disclosure by homeowners on the mandatory disclosure statement.

LATENT DEFECT CASE TIMELINE

- **1920** The house is built

- **1985** The roof on the house is replaced

- **1995** The homeowner buys the house

- **2010** Kitchen ceiling leaks water. Damage to the drywall ceiling is repaired and the damaged wooden flooring is replaced.

- **2014 May 15** The homeowner lists the house for sale.

- **2014 May 30** The purchaser views the house at an open house.

- **2014 May 31** The purchaser makes an offer to purchase, conditional on inspection.

- **2014 June 15** The purchaser inspects alone, without a building inspector, and waives the condition.

- **2014 June 30** The purchaser closes the transaction and takes possession.

- **2015 January 31** Water leaks through the kitchen ceiling causing damage. Purchaser retains Contractor to inspect. Contractor advises that leak originates with a defect in the roof of long-standing. Contractor notes that the ceiling has been repaired before, within the past 10 years.

- **2015 May 15** Purchaser retains Contractor to replace the roof and repair the ceiling damage.

LIST OF WITNESSES

- Alex Homeowner, seller of the home

- Brook Purchaser

- Kim Contractor, Contractor retained by Purchaser

- Leslie Expert, an engineer who practices as a building inspector for residential transactions

LATENT DEFECT WITNESS STATEMENTS

Statement of Alex Homeowner

1. I bought the house at 123 1st Ave. in Ottawa, in 1995.

2. This was my first house purchase. I have no relevant education, training or experience with respect to construction or maintenance of houses.

3. After I purchased the house, I made cosmetic changes. In each case, I hired a suitable trade to do the work. I did not perform any repairs or changes to the roof. I was told by my real estate agent in 1995 that the roof was approximately 10 years old and that roofs of that nature last 20 to 30 years.

4. In the winter of 2010, around February, I noticed water was leaking from the kitchen ceiling. I called a plumber to inspect and repair.

5. The plumber told me that the leak originated in the upper floors, but he could not figure out what was the cause. He told me that it would not happen again and I accepted his advice.

6. I hired another contractor to repair the damage to the drywall in the ceiling. The wood flooring was damaged and I replaced it with ceramic tile that is more suitable for kitchen use.

7. In 2014 I determined to sell the house. I retained a real estate agent, who gave me a form to fill out. This form is attached as Exhibit 1. The relevant section is that the house has not suffered any water damage, which I believed to be true.

8. A few weeks after I listed the house for sale, my agent conducted an open house. A purchaser came to look at the house and made an offer to purchase the next day. After negotiation, I accepted the offer. The offer was conditional upon a building inspection.

9. Nobody asked me any questions about the condition of the house or damage that may have been suffered. The building inspection condition was

later waived, and the transaction closed on schedule June 30, 2014.

10. The next I heard about the house was when I received a demand letter, which is attached as Exhibit 2.

Signed, *Alex Homeowner*

Witness statement of Brook Purchaser

1. I was interested in purchasing a house, such as the one at 123 1st Ave. I looked at several old homes, and actually saw this house in May 2014.

2. The occasion was an open house conducted by a real estate agent with whom I was not familiar. I looked around the house and it seemed fine. I asked about the condition of the property, and the agent showed me a form that was signed by the homeowner and is attached hereto as Exhibit 1.

3. I have no experience purchasing houses and no experience in construction or maintenance. The purchase was made conditional upon the building inspection, on the advice of the real estate agent, who double ended the transaction.

4. I didn't know what a building inspection was, and when I went to see the property two weeks later, I looked around more carefully. I took a couple of hours and took some photographs. Nothing seemed to be out of the ordinary or wrong with the property. The real estate agent was present for the inspection. The agent told me to get a professional to inspect,

but the cost would be as much as $1,000, which I did not want to spend.

5. I waived the building inspection condition and then closed the sale of the property through my lawyer on June 30, 2014. I moved into the house and enjoyed living there.

6. In January 2015, Ottawa underwent a particularly severe winter. It was very cold and then we had a quick thaw. I noticed water was pouring from the kitchen ceiling. I called a contractor, who told me that the cause was a roof defect which allowed water to infiltrate into the attic and then follow the line of some ductwork into the kitchen ceiling. This was completely unexpected. I had relied on the statement by Alex Homeowner.

7. The contractor said that he could not do any work on the roof, which was the source of the problem, until the following spring.

8. In the spring, the contractor told me that it was not worthwhile to repair the roof and that I should replace it altogether. I did so on his advice. He also performed the work to repair the kitchen ceiling. He has told me that the extra cost for replacing the roof as opposed to repairing it, was not that much.

9. I retained a lawyer to send a demand letter to Alex Homeowner, which is attached as Exhibit 2. Exhibit 3 is the invoice from my contractor, Kim Contractor.

Signed, *Brook Purchaser*

Witness statement of Kim Contractor

1. I am a building contractor, with 20 years of experience on the job. I work for residential developers, and homeowners. I do repairs and renovations, and occasionally build a house from start to finish.

2. I was called by Brook Purchaser in January 2015. I was told that there was water pouring into the kitchen from the ceiling.

3. I attended at the house at 123 1st Ave. I saw exactly what I was told by telephone. I cut open the ceiling and determined that water was coming down from the pipes and ducts leading up to the roof. I went into the attic access and saw that the water was coming through the roof from a hole in the roof itself.

4. I covered the hole in the roof with a temporary fix. This stopped the water from infiltrating into the attic. I then installed fans to dry up the water in both the attic and in the kitchen. It took a few days to dry.

5. Because I would have to perform exterior work, I advised the client to wait for the spring to deal with the problem. The roof was very old and it would be far better to replace the roof than to perform repairs now and still have to replace the roof within a few years.

6. I also told the client that this was not the first time that this leak had occurred. It was obvious from looking at the hole in the roof as well as the rusted

area where the water infiltrated through the pipes and ducts, that this happened more than once in the recent past. When I cut into the ceiling in the kitchen, I could see that this had been repaired recently as well. How recently, I could not tell. This is a case of cover-up by the former owner.

7. I told my client that the cost to repair the roof and attic insulation, and to repair the ceiling in the kitchen would be approximately $20,000, evenly split between the roof/attic and the kitchen charges. The cost to replace the roof and repair the ceiling was $25,000. The cost to replace the roof alone was $20,000.

Signed, *Kim Contractor*

Witness statement of Leslie Expert

1. I am a practicing professional engineer, and have been acting as a building inspector for residential clients for more than 10 years.

2. I was asked by Alex Homeowner to inspect 123 1st Ave. The client told me that there was a dispute about whether the purchaser of the property should have discovered the hole in the roof with a diligent inspection.

3. It is my opinion that any prudent inspection should have included the attic. A professional building inspector would certainly have looked into the attic. This was an old house. In spring time, there was no reason to omit this step. From the description of Kim Contractor, the hole in the roof would be

clearly visible to the naked eye of a prudent inspector.

4. I am not surprised that Brook Purchaser, a layperson, missed this problem. That is why professional inspectors are so important.

Signed, *Leslie Expert, P. Eng.*

LATENT DEFECT CASE EXHIBITS

Exhibit 1

Seller warranty disclosure statement

The seller warrants that the following statements are true with respect to the structural integrity of the house:

#14. There has been no infiltration by water into the house from the exterior.

Signed, *Alex Homeowner*

Exhibit 2

Letterhead of Smith Law Firm

June 14, 2015

Alex Homeowner

Re: Sale of 123 1st Ave. to Kim Purchaser

We have been retained by Kim Purchaser in connection with the above-noted purchase transaction. We have been advised by our client that there has been extensive damage caused to the interior of the house by reason of infiltration of water into the attic from the roof.

We are advised that you gave to our client a warranty that there had been no such infiltration. Our client has determined that there had been such infiltration during your ownership. Therefore, we have been instructed to commence an action against you for the damages arising from such infiltration unless you are prepared to settle this matter beforehand.

We ask that you retain counsel and negotiate a resolution of this dispute. Failing this, legal action will proceed.

Yours truly,

Lynn Smith

Exhibit 3

Invoice for services rendered at 123 1st Ave. in January and May, 2015.

Temporary repairs to roof, attic and kitchen in January 2015, including rental of drying equipment.

Removal and replacement of roof. Removal and replacement of insulation in the attic. Removal and replacement of drywall ceiling in the kitchen, and repainting entire kitchen.

Our charges are $26,550 plus applicable sales taxes.

Signed, *Kim Contractor*